# Contents

# Derivation - Word formation

There are three ways of word formation:
  I.   Affixes (Prefixes and Suffixes)
  II.  Conversion
  III. Alternating sounds and stress

## Affixation

**Verbs**

1. Prefix

   **"de-"** gives new meaning to the verb:

   a) Disabling - Приведение в нерабочее состояние.

Activate → deactivate – деактивировать
I would like to deactivate "Windows 10".

   b) Bringing in reverse state. Приведение в обратное состояние.

Compress – сдавливать, сжимать →
decompress – разжать, декомпрессировать
With great difficulty, Jack has decompressed the spring.

Contaminate – заражать → decontaminate – обеззараживать
The company decontaminated the site before decommissioning.

   **"dis-"** turns the verb into an opposite action.

Appear → disappear – исчезать, скрываться
They disappeared round the corner.

Assemble → disassemble – разбирать, демонтировать
We need to disassemble these engines.

Connect → disconnect – отключать, разъединять
Must I disconnect the devices?

**"mis-"** means to do in a wrong way,

Date → misdate – неправильно датировать
My birth certificate was misdated at the passport department.

Direct → misdirect – неверно направлять, вводить в заблуждение. We were lost because Peter misdirected us.

Understand → misanderstand – неправильно понять
I'm afraid you misunderstood what I said.

**"over-"** - something more than an equivalent.

Balance → overbalance – перевесить, выводить из равновесия
Jeff had overbalanced and fell off the ladder.

Load → overloaded – перегружать
The lorry was overloaded; it was dangerous.

Do → overdo – переусердствовать
Don't press too hard; don't overdo.

Heat → overheat – перегреть
You overheated the milk; it's too hot for the baby.

**"un-"** [ʌn] transforms verbs into the opposite action.

Balance → unbalance – лишать душевного равновесия
After the divorce, he was completely unbalanced.

Button → unbutton – расстегивать, чувствовать себя свободно
You can unbutton your coat; it's not too cold here.

Do → undo – отменять
Undo your order, please.

Dress → undress – раздевать(ся)
Can you undress your little sister?

**"under-|"** - not completely done.

Cook → undercook – недоварить
The potato is hard; you undercooked it.

Estimate – оценить → underestimate – недооценить
I underestimated his ability to convince.

2. Suffix

**"-ate"** forms the verbs, saving the meaning of the root.

Accommodate – предоставлять жилье
Some families accommodate foreign students.

Decorate – украшать
The children were decorating the New Year tree.

Dictate – диктовать
Stop dictating to me how to behave.

**"-en"** turns the words into verbs.

Bright → brighten – to make brighter, осветлить, придавать блеск
Please, open the curtains to brighten the room.

Dark → darken – затемнять, темнеть, темнить, омрачать
Please, close the curtains to darken the room.

Light – свет, легкий → lighten – освещать, облегчить
The chandelier will lighten the hall brightly.

Worse → worsen – ухудшать(ся)
The situation worsened from day to day.

Pray, it will lighten your soul.
Молитесь, это облегчит вашу душу.

**"-ify"** [ifai] makes the meaning as indicated in the root.

Electrify – электрифицировать
First of all, we shall electrify these buildings.

Magnify – увеличивать
I need to magnify it; pass me the magnifying glass.

Terrify – ужасать
His idea has terrified me.

**"-ise"** – to do as indicated in the root.

Advertise – рекламировать
All companies advertise their products.

Dramatise – драматизировать
Don't dramatise the events; it's not the end of the world.
Everything will be all right.

Normalise – нормализовать
I am tired of your scandals; you must normalise your
relationships.
You are a normal couple, a good match.

**"-ish"** saves the meaning of the root.

Establish – учреждать, основывать
They decided to establish a new branch of the company.

Furnish – обставить мебелью
I'd like to furnish the lounge with Italian furniture.

Publish – публиковать
They approved her novel and promised to publish it at the
earliest opportunity.

# Nouns

1. Prefix

**"De-"** gives the following meanings to the noun:

    a) Disabling - Приведение в нерабочее состояние.
Activation → deactivation деактивация
The deactivation of the programme was a success.

    b) Bringing in reverse state – обратное состояние.
Cadence → decadence упадок
All countries in every century have their decadence period.

**"dis"** turns the noun to an opposite meaning.

Ability → disability – инвалидность, неспособность
Clare cannot jump because of her disability.

Agreement → disagreement. He was demonstrating his disagreement during the whole discussion.

Charge - заряд → discharge – разрядка
Discharge happened in the electrical circuit (цепь).

**"em-"** / **"en-"** in front of the consonants "b, p, m" – "em-"; in all the rest cases – prefix "en-".

Bank – берег → embankment – набережная
We were walking along the embankment of the Thames.

Couragement → encouragement – поощрение, ободрение
It's always good if a young employee hears your encouragement.

**"mis-"** a) Turns the noun into the opposite meaning.

Fortune → misfortune – несчастье, неудача
Misfortune chases him lately.

Trust → mistrust - недоверие
His words caused my mistrust.

b) Doing in the wrong way.

Understanding → misunderstanding – неправильное понимание, недоразумение. I failed the exam because of a misunderstanding of the technical text.

Nothing happened; it was just a misunderstanding.

**"over"**
a) More than the norm.

Balance → overbalance – перевес, избыток
The result of our economy was overbalanced.

b) What is on the top or above?

Coat → overcoat – верхняя одежда, пальто
Take your overcoat off, you won't feel cold here.

Dose → overdose – передозировка
Overdose was the reason for his collapse.

Time → overtime – сверхурочное время
Janine often works overtime.

**"un"** gives an opposite meaning to the noun.

Certainty → uncertainty – неуверенность, сомнения
The uncertainty didn't allow him to come to a decision.

Predictability– предсказуемость→ unpredictability–
непредсказуемость. Unpredictability is the main feature (главная черта) of his character.

Loading погрузка → unloading – выгрузка
Unloading of the lorry was in full swing (в полном разгаре).

2. Suffix

**"-an"** / **"-ian"** indicates profession or country of origin.

Physician, historian;        American, Russian, Brazilian

**"-ant"** / **"-ent"** form a noun from a verb.

Athlete, decadent, immigrant, student.

**"-ee"** forms nouns, denoting a person (from verbs).

Addressee, employee, grantee, referee.

**"-ism"** - abstract nouns: social flow (movement).

Socialism, capitalism, communism, rasism, collectivism

**"-ment"** turns a verb into a noun.

Achieve → achievement – достижение
The publication of his poems was a great achievement for Robert.

Acknowledge → acknowledgement – признание
At last, he achieved acknowledgment.

Disappoint → disappointment – разочарование
Her betrayal was a real disappointment for Peter.

**"-ness"** turns an adjective into a noun.

Bright → brightness – яркость
The brightness of her talent was admirable.

Exact → exactness – точность
Exactness is the politeness of kings.

Stubborn → stubbornness – упрямство
Lisa's stubbornness is very annoying.

**"-(t)ion"** transforms a verb into a noun.

Examine → examination
I have successfully passed the examination.

Celebrate → celebration – празднование
There were many guests at the celebration of their marriage
 anniversary.

Congratulate → congratulation – поздравление
They have received a lot of congratulations via mail.

Resolute → resolution – резолюция, решение
This resolution is of great importance for them.

**"-ure"** forms a noun from a verb.

Creature – существо, disclosure – раскрытие,
disclosure of the case – раскрытие дела,
ligature – лигатура, pleasure – удовольствие.


## Adjective

1. Prefix

**"anti-"** - aiming against …

Anti-war – against the war – антивоенный
We participated in the anti-war meeting.

Antibody - антитело
After my illness, the antibodies were produced in my blood.

Antifreeze – антифриз
Drivers use antifreeze for their cars in the freezing weather
(морозная погода).

**"auto-"** means self-contained (самостоятельный), automatic.

Autobiography – автобиография
I was asked to write my autobiography.

Autonomous – автономный
The word "autonomous" means independent.

**"de-"**
   a) Disabling

Activated → deactivated – деактивированный
If you have eaten bad food, you need to take deactivated carbon (уголь).
   b) Changing into reverse state

Caffeinated → decaffeinated – без кофеина
Sara likes decaffeinated coffee.

Capsulated → decapsulated – декапсулированный
Henry preferred to take decapsulated medicine.

**"dis-"** gives an opposite meaning to adjectives.

Abled → disabled – нетрудоспособный
Any disabled person needs help, financial support and assistance.

Agreeable → disagreeable – неприятный, сварливый
She felt some disagreeable smell. Tom's disagreeable character let him down (подвел его) this time.

Chargeable → dischargeable – разряжаемый
He found out, that the batteries were dischargeable.

**"extra-"** – a) either after or beyond the regular;
            b) more, than is usually expected;
            c) additional.

Extracurricular – внеклассный, after classes
The vice director was responsible for the extracurricular schedule.

Extraordinary – незаурядный, внеплановый
There were hot debates at that extraordinary meeting.

Extra virgin – of high quality, экстра-класс
Extra virgin olive oil is extracted by cold pressing.

**"inter-"** shows the interaction of something
(взаимодействие).

International – международный
The international forum of young people took place in our town.

Intentional – умышленный, намеренный
It was an intentional murder.

Interchangeable – взаимозаменяемый
I was lucky to buy some interchangeable spare parts.

**"mis-"** - in a wrong way.

Spell-spelled → misspelled – with a spelling mistake
I highlighted your misspelled words.

Miscellaneous – смешанный, возможно перепутать
Today we shall work with some miscellaneous words.

Placed → misplaced – неправильно расположенный
Sue often puts the books in a misplaced order.

**"over-"** forms adjectives with the meaning "above normal".

Bearing → overbearing – властный, повелительный
Sometimes parents are overbearing with their children.

Blown → overblown – непомерно раздутый
He was so proud of himself, looking like an overblown turkey.

Long → overlong – слишком длинный
Their conversation was irritatingly overlong; she lost her temper.

**"post-"** is equivalent to "after".

Postclassical – постклассический
These artists belong to the postclassical period.

Postmeridian – после полудня (p.m.)
Postmeridian – it's the time between noon and midnight:
in the afternoon or evening.

Postoperative – послеоперационный
She was successfully recovering during her postoperative period.

**"un-"** - opposite meaning.

Countable → uncountable – неисчисляемый
We don't use the indefinite article with uncountable nouns.

Economic → uneconomic – неэкономичный
Miss Rosy offered an uneconomic project of building.

Tidy → untidy – неопрятный. Henry is such an untidy boy!

Wealthy – состоятельный → unwealthy – небогатый
Their father was an unwealthy man.

The prefixes, giving a negative meaning to adjectives:

**"in-"**

Secure → insecure – ненадежный, небезопасный
The building appeared to be insecure for accommodating.

**"il-"** - is always in front of "l"

Legal → illegal – нелегальный
He was sure it was an illegal way of doing it.

**"im-"** - in front of consonants "b", "p", "m"

Possible → impossible – невозможный
It was impossible to talk to her.

**"ir-"** In front of "r"

Regular → irregular – неправильный, неравномерный
There are more than one hundred irregular verbs in English.

## 2. Suffix

The suffixes, giving the meaning of possibility to use:

**"-able"**

Countable – исчисляемый, possible to count
Countable nouns are those, which we can count: pens, cats, trees.

**"-ible"**

Edible – съедобный
The porridge she cooked was surprisingly edible.

Flexible – гибкий, уступчивый
His flexible manner of talking helps him to achieve positive results.

**"-en"** indicates the state of an object.

Break → broke → broken – сломанный
Wood → wooden – деревянный
The wooden chair was broken.

**"-ive"** indicates the presence of some quality.

Impressive – впечатляющий
Her over sudden appearance was quite impressive.

Passive – пассивный. Passive voice means that something is done to the subject.

**"-ous"** gives meaning to the root…

Conscious – сознательный, находящийся в сознании
When he came into the ward, the patient was already conscious.

Cautious – осторожный
The cat tried to be very cautious not to spook the mouse.

Famous – знаменитый, прославленный
Richard is a very famous actor.

**"-y"** – to describe a condition, situation, state, etc.

Sun → sunny – солнечный
We had many sunny days during our holidays.

Rain → rainy – дождливый
Cloud → cloudy – облачный
Our excursion was unlucky; the sky was cloudy and the weather was rainy.

### Adverb

1. Prefix

**"over-"**

Time → overtime – сверхурочно
Tom's constant overtime work made him ill.

## "un-"

Commonly → uncommonly – необычно
Tom used the word in this context very uncommonly.

Well → unwell
Sandra couldn't go to work, because she was unwell.

## 2. Suffix

**"–ward(s)"** shows the direction.

Forward – вперед
Hope my offer is acceptable; looking forward to your reply.

Upwards – вверх
I think the shelf is too low, move it upwards a bit.

Downwards – вниз
Where is the lift going? – Downwards.

**"-wise"** shows the direction and position.

Clockwise – по часовой стрелке
You have to massage clockwise.

Anti-clockwise – против часовой стрелки
Slowly twist your leg 5 times clockwise, then 5 times anti-clockwise.

**"-ish"** means "approximately"

Childish – по-детски
It was childish of you to behave like that.

Greenish – зеленоватый
The curtains were beige with a green pattern..

Weakish – слабоват
He started feeling a bit weakish of hunger.

Agree - соглашаться → agreement - согласие, disagree – не соглашаться, agreeable – согласный.

Disagree – не соглашаться → disagreement – несогласие, disagreeable – несогласный

So, we can change the words by adding prefixes and affixes to the root, to change them into other parts of speech or to change their meaning.

## Conversion

1. Verb – Noun

We cannot define to which part of speech the word belongs, out of context. The only orientation is defining by an article or particle "to".

"a / an, the" – a noun; "to" – a verb

a) to microwave – подогревать в микроволновке → a microwave – микроволновка

We bought a new microwave and at once decided to microwave our pizza.

b) to name – называть → a name – имя

Let's name our puppy. – What name are you thinking of? – Rex.

c) to salt – солить → the salt – соль,

Pass me the salt, please; I'd like to salt my soup.

2. Noun – Verb

a) an alert – тревога, сигнал тревоги, боевой готовности to alert – объявлять тревогу, предупреждать об опасности

The radio operator alerted the officer about the forthcoming attack and the officer commanded to announce alert.
Радист предупредил офицера о предстоящем нападении, и тот приказал объявить тревогу.

b) a call – звонок → to call – звонить

Give me a call please. Позвоните мне, пожалуйста. –
I'll call you. Я тебе позвоню.

c) a cover – укрытие, прикрытие → to cover – укрывать

They had to work under the cover.
Им приходилось работать под прикрытием

Please, cover the baby with a blanket.
Пожалуйста, накрой ребенка одеялом.

3. Adjective – Verb

a) clean – чистый → to clean – чистить

If you want your room to be clean, you must clean it.
Если вы хотите, чтобы ваша комната была чистой, вы должны ее убрать.

b) blind – слепой → to blind – ослепить

The unexpected bright light of the car blinded him and he felt himself like a blind helpless man.
Неожиданный яркий свет машины ослепил его, и он почувствовал себя слепым и беспомощным.

4. Adjective – Noun

a) sweet – сладкий → a sweet – сладость, конфета

I don't like chocolate sweets; they are too sweet.
Не люблю шоколадные конфеты; они слишком сладкие.

b)  swimming – плавательный, купальный →
    swimming – плавание, купание

We regularly attend our swimming pool, because we like
swimming.
Мы регулярно ходим в плавательный бассейн, потому что
любим плавание.

c)  kind – добрый → a kind – тип, сорт

Robert is a very kind man; he always helps me to carry my bags.
Роберт очень добрый человек; он всегда помогает мне носить
мои сумки.

What kind of fireplace would you like to buy?
Какого типа камин вы бы хотели купить?

d)  blind – слепой → blinds – жалюзи

Despite he was blind; he was freely moving around the room.
Несмотря на то, что он был слеп; он свободно перемещался
по комнате.

The blinds were always closed in his bedroom.
Жалюзи в его спальне всегда были закрыты.

5.  Noun – Adjective

a)  a dinner – обед + a table – стол

We put these two nouns one after the other; the first noun turns
into an adjective:
We bought a dinner table – Мы купили обеденный стол.

b)  a kitchen – кухня + equipment – оборудование

Ann has got new kitchen equipment.
У Энн новое кухонное оборудование.

c) a school – школа  + a director – директор

The school director ordered a new desk for our class.
Директор школы (школьный директор) заказал для нашего
класса новую парту.

d) a desk – парта, письменный стол + a lamp – лампа

They also delivered a new desk lamp for that desk.
Также они доставили новую настольную лампу для этого
стола.

e) a school – школа + a daybook – дневник

My parents check my school daybook every weekend.
Мои родители проверяют мой школьный дневник каждые
выходные.

6. Preposition – Noun

preposition "up" – вверх → noun – взлет
preposition "down" – вниз → noun – падение

Robert was disappointed with his career last years:
his ups and downs were very irritating.
Роберт был разочарован своей карьерой в последние годы:
его взлеты и падения очень раздражали.

7. Conjunction – Noun

a) but – но

Den, you must wash the dishes today. – But I am busy,
dad. – No "buts", you have to help our mother.
Ден, ты должен сегодня помыть посуду. - Но я занят, папа.
Никаких "но", ты должен помочь нашей маме.

b) if – если

I will wash the dishes if you ….. –
No "ifs". Look, I am clearing everything in the cupboard.
Our mum is overtired this week.

Я вымою посуду, если ты… .. -
Никаких "если". Смотри, я разбираю всё в шкафу.
Наша мама на этой неделе переутомилась.

    c)  and – и

I will read my book and listen to music and dance. –
Don't use "and" many times. Better to say:  I will read my book,
listen to music and dance. – OK, mummy, thank you.

Я буду читать свою книгу и слушать музыку, и танцевать. –
Не используй "и" много раз. Лучше сказать: я буду читать
свою книгу, слушать музыку и танцевать. – Хорошо,
мамочка, спасибо.

### Alternating letters (sounds)

alternaiting – перемежающийся

   1.  Verb – Noun

  a)  to advise [z] –советовать, консультировать,
      рекомендовать; (verb)
      an advice  [s]– совет (noun)

I would advise you to ask his forgiveness.
Я бы посоветовал вам попросить у него прощения.

Could you advise us on how to work with this device?
Не могли бы вы проконсультировать, как работать с этим
устройством?

Can you advise the best route to London?
Вы можете порекомендовать лучший маршрут до Лондона?

I am very uncertain about the choice; I need your advice.
Я не очень уверен в своем выборе; мне нужен твой совет.

     b) to believe – верить; (verb)
       belief – вера (noun)

It can't be the truth, I don't believe you.
Это не может быть правдой, я тебе не верю.

His belief saved his life.
Его вера спасла ему жизнь.

     c)  to practise – упражняться
     practice – практика, применение

You need to practise your pronunciation daily.
Вы должны ежедневно практиковать свое произношение.

The gained experience will help you during your practice.
Приобретённый опыт поможет вам во время практики.

     d)  to express – выражать
     an express – экспресс = a fast train

Express your thoughts clearly.
Четко выражайте свои мысли.

To get from St. Petersburg to Moscow quicker, you need to take an express.
Чтобы быстрее добраться из Санкт-Петербурга в Москву, нужно сесть на экспресс.

    2.  Noun – Noun

    `desert – пустыня → de`ssert – десерт

# Changing syllable stress
## Изменение слогового ударения

a) to ob`ject – возражать (verb)
   an `object – объект (noun)

Do not even object; we made this decision together with your mum.
Даже не возражайте; мы приняли это решение вместе с вашей мамой.
The new construction object is not approved.
Новый объект строительства не утвержден.

b) to pre`sent – представлять, дарить (verb)
   a `present – подарок (noun)
   `present – нынешний, настоящее время (adjective)

William will present our company at the briefing.
Уильям представит нашу компанию на брифинге.

What shall we present to your mother at our first meeting? –
I suppose flowers will be enough.
Что мы подарим твоей маме при первой встрече? -
Полагаю, цветов будет достаточно.

We must find a nice present for her birthday.
Надо найти ей хороший подарок на день рождения.

It's difficult to use the present indefinite tense correctly at the very beginning.
Вначале трудно использовать настоящее неопределенное время правильно.

I am having lunch at present time. Я сейчас обедаю.

# Word abbreviation

Common words, that are officially used in English:

Advertisement → "ad" – рекламное объявление
I would like to place an ad in your newspaper.

Bicycle → "bike" – велосипед
Henry cares about his bike as if it is his child.

Influenza → "flu" – грипп
I am sneezing and running high temperature; perhaps it's flu.

Professional → "pro" – профессионал
Richard is the best in our department; he is a real pro.

Television → "TV", "telly" – телевидение, телик
Sue spent the whole day, sitting in front of the telly.
She adores watching different TV programmes.

Vegetables → "veg" – овощи
Mainly I eat fruit and veg.

Small dog → "doggie" – собачка
Oh, look at that cute doggie!

Asap = as soon as possible (usually in email or messages)

# Parts of speech

## Articles

Any article is the indicator of the noun.

The word or word combination, following the article, is either a noun or an adjective + a noun.

"a / an" + noun
"a / an" + adjective + noun
"the" + noun
"the" + adjective + noun

The basic difference between "a / an" and "the" is:

"a / an" is the Indefinite article. We use it if we mention a noun in a conversation for the first time.

"a / an" denotes one, any, any of many; a subject unknown to us, about which we did not know yet.

The Indefinite article "a / an" is used only with singular nouns.

It's a new toy. I have a new coat. There is a cat here.

If we know what noun we are talking about, then we can insert the Definite article "the".

The Definite article "the" is used with singular and plural objects.

I have bought a car. Tomorrow I am going to bring the car home. All the cars at the shop are of high quality.

In addition to what we already know:

**We use the Indefinite article "a / an" with:**

1.  words and phrases indicating quantity: a couple – пара; a dozen – дюжина; a few – немного, несколько; a little – немного, слегка; a hundred – сотня, a great deal of – много.

2.  before proper nouns in the meaning of "unfamiliar", "some" or "someone".

    A Lucy, by the door, would like to see you.
    Какая-то Люси, у двери, хотела бы вас видеть.

3.  before abstract nouns, when they have the meaning of a special quality.

    An idea came to my mind. Мне пришла в голову идея.

4.  in exclamations before singular countable nouns after words: as – в качестве, как; quite – совсем, довольно; such – такой; what – какой , что за.

As a representative of the company, I insist on the talks.
Как представитель компании, я настаиваю на переговорах.

I suppose it's quite a good idea.
Полагаю, это вполне хорошая (неплохая) идея.

Alice is such a wonderful girl.
Алиса такая замечательная девушка.

What a pretty baby he is! Какой хорошенький малыш!

What an amazing couple they are. Какая потрясающая пара.

5. before nouns in the singular, in the expression "there is…":

There is a new sofa in the lounge. В гостиной новый диван.

6.    in phrases used to express the ratio (соотношение):

We have to eat four times a day.
Мы должны есть четыре раза в день.

I go to college 5 days a week.
Я хожу в колледж 5 дней в неделю.

Toby was driving 80 kilometres an hour.
Тоби ехал со скоростью 80 километров в час.

We bought nice apples 3 pounds per kilo, but usually
they cost 2 pounds a kilo.
Мы купили хорошие яблоки по 3 фунта за килограмм,
но обычно они стоят 2 фунта килограмм.


**We use the Definite article "the" in the below cases**:

1.   before nouns that have a definition:

The new student in our group was very shy.
Новый ученик в нашей группе очень стеснялся.

The professor of our university has got the grant.
Профессор нашего университета получил грант.

The clouds in the sky are becoming darker.
Облака в небе становятся темнее.

2. before nouns denoting the names of:

rivers – the Thames, the Enisey, the Voga
seas – the Irish Sea, the Baltic Sea, the Black Sea
oceans – the Pacific Ocean, the Atlantic Ocean
mountains – the Alps, the Ural Mountains, the Andes
books – "The War and Peace", "The Moonstone"
newspapers – "The Times", "The Pravda"
ship names – "The Titanic", "The Amazon Beauty"

3. with the adjectives: last, next, only, same, very

last – последний
In the last lesson, the students worked well.
На последнем занятии студенты добились успеха.

next – следующий
The next stop is "Baker Street".
Следующая остановка – "Бейкер-стрит".

only – единственный
You are the only girl that I adore.
Ты единственная девушка, которую я обожаю.

same – одинаковый, тот же самый
The chairs should be of the same colour.
Стулья должны быть одного цвета.

The chairs should be of the same colour as the sofa.
Стулья должны быть того же цвета, что и диван.

very – самый, тот самый, самый предельный
Ann is the very woman I want to marry.
Энн - та самая женщина, на которой я хочу жениться.

Go to the very end of the tunnel.
Идите в самый конец туннеля.


## We do not use the Definite article "the":

1. with the names of the towns, squares and streets;
    London, Moscow; Trafalgar Square, Piccadilly Circus;
    St. Johns Street, I live in Baker Street

2. with the names and titles of people:
    Patrick, Maurine, Mr. Brown, Mrs. Dean, Miss Flint

3. with the names of months and days of week:
   Sunday, on Monday; January, in March, in August

4. with the names of sciences, abstract nouns and subjects:
   I like history.
   She felt homesickness (тоску по дому).
   We speak English.

5. with the names of meals:
   I have toasts for breakfast. It's teatime. Yesterday we had dinner at the restaurant and light supper at home.

## Prepositions

### "about" – о, об, около

Jill was thinking about this work. Джилл думала об этой работе.

I have no idea what you are talking about.
Понятия не имею, о чем вы говорите.

Father has come home at about 5 o'clock.
Отец пришел домой около 5 часов.

### "along" – вдоль

I like to wander along the small old streets of our town.
Я люблю бродить по маленьким старинным улочкам города.

Put these ornaments along the whole perimeter.
Прикрепите эти украшения по всему периметру.

### "among" – среди

I have found my kitten among the cushions.
Я нашла своего котенка среди подушек.

We found that small old house among new high buildings.
Мы нашли этот небольшой старинный дом среди новых высотных зданий.

**"across"** – через

A new bridge was erected across the river.
Новый мост был возведен через реку.

Lookout while walking across the road.
Будьте осторожны, переходя дорогу.

When we travel by plane, we fly across the ocean.
Когда путешествуем на самолете, мы летаем через океан.

**"around"** – вокруг, по

While walking around the town, I took many photographs.
Прогуливаясь по городу, я сделал много фотографий.

Look around. What do you see?
Посмотри вокруг! Что ты видишь?

A new road is being constructed around the village.
Вокруг села строится новая дорога.

**"because of"** – из-за

Because of our quarrel, we wasted a lot of time.
Из-за нашей ссоры мы потеряли много времени.

She lost the job because of her laziness.
Она потеряла работу из-за своей лени.

**"below"** – ниже, под

My armchair is right below the portrait.
Мое кресло прямо под портретом.

Ann's flat is below mine.
Квартира Энн под моей.

**"beside"** – рядом, рядом с, возле

Our houses are beside each other.
Наши дома рядом.

The coffee table is beside the sofa.
Журнальный столик рядом с диваном.

The bread shop is beside my house.
Хлебная лавка возле моего дома.

**"besides"** – кроме, помимо

There are many others besides me, who disagree with you.
Кроме меня, есть много других, кто с вами не согласен.

I won't walk; I'm tired and besides, it's raining
Я не пойду; Я устала и к тому же идет дождь

**"between"** – между

The sofa was between the window and the armchair.
Диван стоял между окном и креслом.

I hope our talk is between us.
Я надеюсь, что наш разговор между нами.

**"beyond"** – more than, вне, за
His home is about four miles beyond Oxford.
Его дом находится примерно в четырех милях за Оксфордом.

The woods go far ahead two miles beyond the river.
Лес уходит вперед на две мили за реку.

He loves her beyond measure. Он любит ее безмерно.

**"by"** – to say what type of transport we use.

I go to work by bus or by trolleybus.
На работу езжу на автобусе или троллейбусе.

I go by car to my summer residence.
На дачу езжу на машине.

To get to another town I go by plane.
Чтобы попасть в другой город, я летаю на самолете.

**"down"** – вниз, вниз по

The group of alpinists was slowly going down the peak.
Группа альпинистов медленно спускалась с вершины.

Jinny was running down the stairs this morning and sprained her ankle. Этим утром Джинни сбегала по лестнице и подвернула лодыжку.

**"from"** – из, от, с

Laura was coming back from the party.
Лаура возвращалась с вечеринки.

She came back from her friends'. Она вернулась от друзей.

Camela returned from her business trip.
Камела вернулась из командировки.

**"in"** – in the expressions:

**"in my way"** – у меня на дороге, мешает, помеха

I cannot get to the door; this huge box is in my way. Я не могу подойти к двери; эта огромная коробка мешает мне.

"in my own way" – по моему, по-своему
My stubborn son listens to my advice but acts in his own way.
Мой упрямый сын слушает мои советы, но действует по-своему.

**"in front of"** – перед, напротив

Their block of flats is right in front of the supermarket.
Их многоквартирный дом находится прямо напротив супермаркета.

Clare was sitting in front of the telly when I came in.
Когда я вошел, Клара сидела перед телевизором.

**"in the middle (of)"** – в центре, в середине

There is a handmade carpet in the middle of the room.
В середине комнаты ковер ручной работы.

Suddenly the tool stopped in the middle of the work.
Вдруг станок остановился посреди работы.

**"inside"** – в, внутри, внутрь

Put the puppy inside the box. Положи щенка в коробку.
The puppy is inside the box now. Щенок сейчас внутри коробки.

**"nearby"** – рядом, близ

My house is nearby the park. – Мой дом рядом с парком.
The shop is situated nearby the church.
Магазин находится близ церкви.

**"next (to)"** – рядом, около

The girl is sitting next to her mum.
Девушка сидит рядом с мамой.

Put the box next to the door.
Поставь ящик около двери.

I want Liz to sit next to me.
Я хочу, чтобы Лиз села рядом со мной.

While walking outside, blind men need the dog to be next to them.
Во время прогулки слепым людям необходимо, чтобы собака находилась рядом с ними.

**"on"** – in the expressions:

"on the way" – по пути, по дороге

Yes, it will be on my way. – Да, мне это будет по пути.
      Grab a chair on your way. Захвати стул по дороге.

**"on the way home"**

On the way home, I'll stop by the shop.
По дороге домой, я заскочу в магазин.

**"on the left of"** – слева от

Can you see that building on the left of the university?
Вы видите то здание слева от университета?

**"on the right of"** – справа от
On the right of our school, there is a library.
Справа от нашей школы находится библиотека.

**"on my left"** – слева от меня

There is a newly built swimming pool on your left.
Слева от вас недавно построенный бассейн.

**"on my right"** – справа от меня

You can see a row of old fashion cottages on my right.
Справа от меня вы видите ряд старинных коттеджей.

**"to the left"** – влево / **"to the right"** – вправо

Look first to the left, then to the right; there are beautiful rows of blossoming magnolia on both sides.
Посмотрите сначала влево, затем вправо;
с обеих сторон красивые ряды цветущих магнолий.

**"off"** – с, со, от

Take your coat off the hanger. Снимите пальто с вешалки.
Take your feet off the table. Убери ноги со стола.
Switch the radio off at the socket.
Отключите радио от розетки.

**"opposite"** – напротив, против

They were sitting opposite the owner of the company.
Они сидели напротив владельца компании.

New bungalows have been built opposite ours.
Новые бунгало построены напротив наших.

**"out of"** – из

Take the cups out of the box, please.
Выньте, пожалуйста, чашки из коробки.

The puppy was trying to get out of the box.
Щенок пытался выбраться из коробки.

He saw a young girl, ready to jump out of the window.
Он увидел молодую девушку, готовую выпрыгнуть из окна.

**"outside"** – у, вне, за пределами

My neighbor always parks his car outside the road.
Мой сосед всегда паркует машину у дороги.

Her husband was standing outside the window, waiting for the moment, when he would be able to see his newborn baby.
Ее муж стоял за окном, ожидая момента, когда он сможет увидеть своего новорожденного младенца.

The aircraft disappeared outside the visibility.
Самолет скрылся за пределами видимости.

### "over" – над

There is a new glass bridge over the river.
Над речкой установлен новый стеклянный мост.

We have hung a crystal chandelier over the round table.
Над круглым столом мы повесили хрустальную люстру.

### "past" – мимо, после

The bus goes past our house.
Автобус проезжает мимо нашего дома.

What's the time, please? – It's half-past two. Который час?
Скажи, пожалуйста – Сейчас половина третьего.

Don't go past. – Не проходи мимо.

### "round" – вокруг, за

The bus stop is round the corner.
Автобусная остановка находится за углом.

After this junction, there should be a roundabout, so we can reverse.
После этого перекрестка должен быть круговой перекресток (кольцо), так что мы можем повернуть обратно.

**"through"** – через, сквозь

Go along the road through the forest and you'll see the village.
Идите по дороге через лес и вы увидите деревню.

At the arrival, we passed through the passport control and
received our +luggage. По прилету, мы прошли через
паспортный контроль и получили багаж.

Mosquitoes have flown through the window.
Комары залетели сквозь окно.

**"up"** – вверх по

The tourists were so tired, that could hardly walk up the hill.
Туристы так устали, что еле поднимались по холму.
Her painful knees don't allow her to walk up the stairs.
Больные колени не позволяют ей подниматься по лестнице.
Do not climb up the ladder, it's not stable.
Не поднимайтесь по стремянке, она неустойчивая.

# Conjunctions

### "although" – хотя

I was joking, although deep in my heart I felt emptiness and sadness.
Я шутил, хотя в глубине души чувствовал пустоту и грусть.

### "though" – хотя, однако

Though the sun was shining brightly, it was a bit cool.
Хотя солнце светило ярко, было немного прохладно.

Sue was sure the decision was correct, though she hesitated about it.
Сью была уверена, что решение было правильным, однако колебалась.

### "even though" – very strong contrast – хотя

He smiled at work, even though he had buried his mother the other day. Он улыбался на работе, хотя на днях похоронил свою мать.

Helen tried to be very polite, even though she felt an awful irritation.
Хелен старалась быть очень вежливой, хотя чувствовала ужасное раздражение.

Even though funds were available, they refused to pay our expenses.
Несмотря на то, что средства были в наличии, они отказались оплачивать наши расходы.

### "despite" – несмотря на

Despite they were married, they lived separately.
Несмотря на то, что они были женаты, они жили отдельно.

The toys were not in great demand despite they were attractive.
Несмотря на свою привлекательность, игрушки не пользовались большим спросом.

**"in spite of"** – несмотря на -

They went out in spite of the strong wind.
Они вышли, несмотря на сильный ветер.

She loved him in spite of all his negative features.
Она любила его, несмотря на все его отрицательные черты.

The weather was lovely in spite of the frost.
Несмотря на мороз, погода стояла прекрасная.

**"if"** – если, если бы

We shall be there in time if we catch the nearest train.
Мы успеем вовремя, если сядем на ближайший поезд.

If you studied grammar, you would pass the exam.
Если бы ты учила грамматику, ты бы сдала экзамен.

**"while"** – пока, в то время как, тогда как

Suzy was meeting Michael at the station, while he was already home.  Сюзи встречала с Майкла на вокзале, в то время как он был уже дома.

While watching television, granny was knitting something.
Бабушка что-то вязала в то время, как она смотрела телевизор.

My wife decided not to go out while I was going to do shopping.
Моя жена решила не выходить на улицу, тогда как я собирался сделать покупки.

**"as long as"** – пока, до тех пор, при условии

I will go with you as long as you will buy the tickets.
Я поеду с тобой, при условии, что ты купишь билеты.

As long as I live, I will never go there again.
Пока жив, больше туда не поеду.
As long as I am working, I shall have some money.
Пока я работаю, деньги у меня будут.

**"unless"** – пока не, если не

except under the circumstances – за исключением случаев,
когда, except on the condition that – за исключением того, что

The kids will stay at home unless they have finished their tasks
before we leave. Дети останутся дома, если не закончат своё
задание до нашего отъезда.

She'll divorce you unless you stop drinking so much. Она
разведется с вами, если вы не перестанете так много пить.

You will be refused any credit unless you pay your bills.
Вам будет отказано в кредите, пока не оплатите свои счета.

**"whether"** – ли

a) to introduce an indirect question

I'd like to know whether you told her the truth or not.
Я хотел бы знать, сказали вы ей правду или нет.

b) a clause after a verb expressing

He doesn't know whether Sarah is in Britain or she's gone to
France. Он не знает, находится ли Сара в Великобритании
или уехала во Францию.

c) implying doubt or choice

You'll eat all of that whether you like it or not.
Ты все это съешь, нравится тебе это или нет.

It's up to you whether to take a day off now or next week. Вам решать, взять выходной сейчас или на следующей неделе.

**"therefore"** – следовательно, поэтому

a) to introduce a logical conclusion from that fact or reason, or as a result

These people opened their umbrellas; therefore it started raining. Эти люди открыли свои зонтики; следовательно, пошел дождь.

b) as a consequence (последствие)

Tom was preoccupied with his problems, therefore he could not help me. Том был озабочен своими проблемами, поэтому не мог мне помочь.

**"however"** – тем не менее, однако

Suzy was a very talented dancer, however she wasn't chosen by the jury. Сюзи была очень талантливой танцовщицей, однако жюри ее не выбрали.

John wasn't rich, however, he invited Lorens to the luxury restaurant.Джон был небогат, тем не менее он пригласил Лоренс в роскошный ресторан.

We inherited a wonderful house, however we preferred to stay in our flat. Мы унаследовали чудесный дом, однако мы предпочли остаться в своей квартире.

**"as well as"** – так же, как и

Our neighbors, as well as our family, prefer calm quiet evenings.
Наши соседи, как и наша семья, предпочитают спокойные тихие вечера.

She is perfect in dancing as well as singing.
Она прекрасно танцует, также как и поет.

**"that"** – что, чтобы

He told his mother that the teacher wanted to see her.
Он сказал своей матери, что учительница хотела ее видеть.

He promised that he would never ever do that again.
Он пообещал, что больше никогда, никогда этого не сделает.

The elderly couple, that were walking along the alley, seemed to be  familiar to me. Пожилая пара, что прогуливалась по аллее, показалась мне знакомой.

**"then"** – впрочем, затем

Lizzy was a bit upset, then she saw Andy, and felt more relaxed.
Лиззи немного расстроилась, затем она увидела Энди и почувствовала себя более расслабленной.

OK, I agree to lend you a large amount, … then I can change my mind.
Хорошо, я согласен одолжить вам большую сумму; ... впрочем я могу и передумать.

**"either…or"** – или ... или,  либо… либо

Either me or Sue! Decide. – Либо я, либо Сью! Решай.
Shall we go at last, or we'll stay at home? Either one or the other.
Пойдем мы наконец, или останемся дома? - Или то, или другое.

**"neither... nor"** – ни … ни

Neither I nor Colin wanted to go out that night.
Ни Коллин, ни я не хотели выходить на улицу в ту ночь.
Nobody wanted to play; neither girls nor boys.
Никто не хотел играть; ни девочки, ни мальчики.

**"when"** – когда

When you go out, close the window and lock the door.
Когда уходишь, закрывай окно и запирай дверь.

When I get home this evening, I am going to have a shower.
Когда я вернусь домой вечером, я собираюсь принять душ.

When we decide to go to the forest, I shall tell you.
Когда мы решим пойти в лес, я вам скажу.

**"whenever"** – в любое время

When shall we start? – Whenever you are ready.
Когда мы начнем? – В любое время как вы готовы.

Whenever I see her, she is always in good mood.
В любое время, как ее вижу, она всегда в хорошем
настроении.

When shall we go to the theatre? – Whenever, as soon as a new
play is on.
Когда мы пойдем в театр? – В любое время, как только будет
новый спектакль.

**"so am I"** = me too - я тоже (agreement)

I am happy. – So am I.
I am working. – So am I.
I was late for work today. – So was John.
My kitten is fluffy. -  And so is mine.

Lisa can speak English. – So can Terry.
My mum works at school. – So does mine.
We saw a new comedy. – So did we.
The Smiths will go to France soon. – So will I.
I have finished the task. – So has Tracey.
Ann would like some water. – So would Liz.

**"Neither am I"** = I am not either - Я тоже не …
Neither do I - I do not either - Я тоже не …
Neither have I - I have not either - Я тоже не …
(disagreement)

I am not mad. - Neither am I.
He isn't sleeping. - Neither am I.
I don't feel hot. - Neither do we.
I haven't got a key. – Neither have I.
Ann can't cook. – Neither can Tom.
I never go to the cinema. – Neither do I. = Nor do I
I won't be here tomorrow – Neither will Betsy.
I am not married. – Nor am I. = Neither am I.
I can't skate – Nor can Henry. = Neither can Henry.
I haven't finished the task. – Neither has Tracey.
My parents aren't going abroad. – Neither are mine.
My mum doesn't work at home. – Nor does mine.
We didn't see this film. – Neither did we.

# Nouns

## Singular nouns

1.  Uncountable nouns: water, milk, sugar, butter, salt, coffee

I like having coffee with a lot of milk.
Я люблю кофе с большим количеством молока.

A lot of salt and sugar is not good for your health.
Большое количество соли и сахара вредно для здоровья.

2.  Abstract nouns: beauty, love, kindness, learning

For all my life, I've been warmed by his love and kindness.
Всю жизнь меня согревали его любовь и доброта.

There is never a lot of kindness. Много доброты не бывает.

3.  Such nouns as information, knowledge and progress, also are always singular.

The progress in our production depends on new technology.
Прогресс в нашем производстве зависит от новых технологий.

The more information you get, the better knowledge you have.
Чем больше информации вы получаете, тем больше у вас знаний.

4.  The word "money" is also always singular, though we can count money; but we count coins and banknotes.

How much money is remaining after our shopping? – Enough cash for your favourite cake. Сколько денег осталось после наших покупок? - Достаточно наличных на твой любимый торт.

5. The word "fruit"

a) If we mean "фрукты" in common, we say:
I like fruit. – Я люблю фрукты.

b) In case of different types:

There were many different kinds of fruit on the table.
На столе было много разных фруктов.

c) Or one single piece:

I will put a piece of fruit into your lunch box, an apple perhaps.
Я положу тебе в ланч-бокс фруктик, яблочко, пожалуй.

3. The word "news"

Although it's in the plural, we can use it as plural and singular.

Do you have any news? - Есть какие-либо новости?
I have some good news. - У меня хорошая новость.

4. Some species of animals: deer, fish, sheep, swine

Yesterday I saw two deer in the reserve.
Вчера в заповеднике я видел двух оленей.

Dad brought three big fish.
Папа принес трех больших рыб.

My father is a farmer; he has four cows, ten sheep and twelve
swine. Мой отец - фермер; у него четыре коровы, десять овец
и двенадцать свиней.

# Plural nouns

Compound nouns have a different formation of plural:

a) Ordinary compound nouns (two-three words together).

Noun + "-s" / "-es" (we add it to the last word).

a pencase → pencases – пеналы
a chatterbox → chatterboxes – болтуны

b) Compound nouns with preposition:

We added the "-s" ending to the first word.

brother-in-law – шурин, деверь → brothers-in-law
son-in-law – зять → sons-in-law

c) Nouns, borrowed from foreign languages, form the plural according to their native languages.

basis – основа → bases – основы
radius – радиус → radii –радиусы

d) Nouns, meaning paired objects are plural:

binoculars – бинокль
glasses (spectacles) – очки
scales – весы
scissors – ножницы
trousers (jeans) – брюки
pants – штаны, underpants - кальсоны, трусы

e) The following nouns are used only in plural:

clothes – одежда
contents – содержание, оглавление
riches – богатства, сокровища
goods — товары      (there are eleven of such nouns totally)

f) "people" has several meanings:

1.    "people" = "люди" – more than one person.

My friends are very honest and kind people.
Мои друзья очень честные и добрые люди.

At the party, I acquainted with some new people.
На вечеринке я познакомился с новыми людьми.

2.    "people" = "народ, народность", the representatives of a
      certain group with the same race, nationality or ethnicity.

The population of India consists predominantly of Indian people.
Население Индии состоит преимущественно из индийцев.

Russian people are remarkably patriotic and enthusiastic. Русские
люди необычайно патриотичны и полны энтузиазма. =
Русский народ необычайно патриотичен и полон энтузиазма.

3.    If we mean several groups of people from multiple racial,
      national or ethnic, backgrounds, we use plural "peoples".

Very many different peoples live in America.
В Америке живет очень много разных народов.

In England, you can meet many peoples from different countries, who
come to language schools for studying English. В Англии можно
встретить множество людей из разных стран, которые
приезжают в языковые школы для изучения английского языка.

So: We use singular form "people" means "люди" = "народ".
Plural "peoples" means "народы" = народности.

# Few – Little

The words "few" and "little" can function as adjectives, adverbs or nouns. As quantifiers, "few" and "little" mean "some".

"many / few" are quantifiers for countable nouns.
"much / little" are quantifiers for uncountable nouns.

## Few – a few (with countable nouns)

"a few" = "some" (but not very many) is a positive idea.

A few people know this. (there are indeed some)
Last night I wrote a few letters. We're going away for a few days.
Are there any pens here? – Yes, a few. – That's enough.
I've got a few friends, so I'm not lonely.
I can't talk to you now. I've got a few things to do.

"few" = not many at all – is a negative idea – nearly no.

Few people know this. (hardly anyone knows this)
There were few people in the park. It was nearly empty.
Your English is good. You make very few mistakes.
I'm sad and I'm lonely. I've got few friends.

## Little – a little (with uncountable nouns)

"a little" – is a positive idea – some but not much.

They have a little money, so they're not poor.
I've got a little money and I am very glad.
There was a little food in the fridge, so we had something to eat.

"little" - is a negative idea - nearly no, nearly nothing.
They have little money. They are very poor.
There was little food in the fridge; it was nearly empty; we had nothing to eat.
I eat very little meat. I don't like it very much.

# Gender

There are four types of gender in English:
masculine, feminine, neuter and common.

We have studied the three of them: masculine, feminine
and neuter.

    1.  Masculine is equal to "he" – "он"

Father, a man, a son, a boy, a brother
Who is the elderly man in the armchair? – He is Tom's grandfather.

    2.  Feminine is equal to "she" – "она"

Mother, a woman, a daughter, a girl, a sister
I have never seen that girl. Who is she? – She is Laura, my sister.

    3.  Neuter is equal to "it" – "он", "она", "оно"

A ball, a college, a dog, fire, a lamp, a house, a tree, a university
What kind of lamp is it? – It is a bedside lamp.

    4.  Common gender includes nouns, which can be both: either masculine or feminine.

An animal, a baby, a child, a friend, a neighbour, an owner, a parent, a person.

Liz has a newborn baby. – Is it a boy or a girl? – It's a girl.

There is a new neighbour in the next-door flat.
Is that a man or a woman? – I haven't seen anyone yet.

I have a new partner. – Is it a he-partner or a she-partner?
It's a very polite middle-aged man. That's all I know so far.

5. Talking about ships, English people call them "she".

The language row over "female" ships. Despite the debates, the Royal Navy is not going to change this tradition. Boats, sailing vessels, liners, cruisers are of the feminine gender.

I shipped aboard a "Liverpool" liner. She was quite comfortable.

6. Cars are also often embodied in female images.

I see you have bought a new "Jaguar" car. –
Oh, yes. When I saw the car, I fell in love with her.

7. Referring to planets and countries as to a female is not only in English but in many other languages as well.

Mother Earth, Mother Nature and Motherland are symbols of the life-giving and life-sustaining beginning.

8. Some nouns, like "war", expressing force, power or destruction, are masculine.

9. The rule about neuter gender in the first book says that we use the pronoun "it", referring to animals.

Talking about domestic animals or pets, we often use "she" or "he", depending on their sex.

I haven't come to you for long. Look at your dog!
He has become so big! – Он стал таким большим!

What's the name of such a cute puppy? –
Как зовут такого милого щенка?
It's a girl. She is Betsy.

# Verb -Tenses

In the first book we have studied:
present, past and future simple tenses;
present, past and future indefinite tenses;
present, past and future continuous tenses
and present perfect tense.

Now we shall move on to more complicated tenses (advanced level).

## Past Perfect Tense

We use the past perfect tense to show that one action was completed before another action in the past.

Мы используем the past perfect tense, чтобы показать, что одно действие в прошлом было выполнено раньше другого.

Действие закончено до определённого момента в прошлом.

We used the auxiliary verb "have" in the present perfect tense.

The auxiliary verb "have" turns into "had" in the past perfect tense. The formula of the past perfect is:

> Noun/ pronoun + had + Participle II

The brigade had completed it before yesterday.

At last her son had fallen asleep and Suzy turned the light off.
*First event* – the son had fallen asleep – past perfect.
*Second event* - Suzy turned the light off – past indefinite.
The son had fallen asleep **before** Suzy turned the light off.

We had approached the gate a minute earlier than the parade started.
She told me, that she had received the best present in her life on that birthday.

"when" + Past Indefinite

He had done it when we came.

We usually use the words "before" or "after"

He lost his temper <u>after</u> he had heard such rude words towards him.

I had changed the coffee in the teacher's lounge <u>before</u> the staff came.
The staff came <u>after</u> I had changed the coffee.

*Let's play with the pairs of sentences and see how the gist (суть) is changing. Compare the time of the actions and think of the difference.*

1. They arrived at the railway station. The train left.
They arrived at the railway station before the train left. –
They were in time.
They arrived at the railway station after the train left. –
They were late.

2. We came home. They delivered our new furniture.
We came home before they delivered our new furniture.
We came home after they delivered our new furniture.

The party had been over before our parents appeared.
The party was over after our parents had appeared.

You can use any past tense after the past perfect.

I was terribly upset after he had shouted at me.
The woman was bitterly crying after her child had been stolen.
They went away after they had collected all the spare parts.

Negative form: had not (hadn't) + Participle II

He had not taken the keys before he closed the door.
Betsy hadn't broken her leg, but she cried loudly.
You hadn't washed your hands, but you came to the table.

Questions:

1. Auxiliary verb "had" + noun/pronoun + Participle II

Had they done the test? - Yes, they had / No, they hadn't yet.

Had she gone home before Christmas? – No, there were no tickets on those days. She went after.

2. Question word + "had" + noun/pronoun + Participle II

When had they done the test? – By 2 o'clock.

Where had she gone before Christmas? – She had come to our hotel to celebrate Christmas and then she went home.

What had you done to her that she cried in the evening? – I had broken her doll, but I apologized after. I promised to buy a new one.

What kind of refurbishing had the Blades made before they moved into their new house? – They redecorated the bedrooms, repaired the fireplace in the lounge and renewed the kitchen.

Who had you talked to before the conference? – To the chairman.

Whom had you met before our lesson? – Our new student, whom I accompanied to the laboratory.

Who had invited you to the theatre? – William had; we went there the same evening.

# Future Perfect Tense

Future Perfect Tense expresses the action we think about
as completed at some point or until a moment in the future.

Future Perfect Tense выражает действие, о котором мы думаем
как о завершенном в какой-то момент или до момента в
будущем.

We use the auxiliary verb "shall/will" indicating the future tense
and "have" pointing to the completion of the action.

> Shall (will) have + Participle II
> Shall (will) have = I'll have

I will have spoken. = I'll have spoken.

We usually use the prepositions "by, before, until"

I will have completed the timetable by 2 o'clock.
He will have done the task by lunchtime.
We shall have gone before your parents come.
They will have finished the exercise by the end of the lesson.

Negative form:

> will not have done = won't have done = 'll not

They won't have finished their discussion until you interfere.
They'll not have finished their discussion until you interfere.
Они не закончат обсуждение, пока вы не вмешаетесь.

I think Peter will not have got the prize. (приз не достанется)
I am sure Rozy won't have bought such a bright dress.
I know them well; they'll not have divorced. (они не разведутся)

"I will have done + when"

> I will have done + when + verb in the present tense

I will have spoken to Nick when he is ready.

He will have done everything when we come.
They will have brought new furniture when they move into the flat.

Questions:

Will + noun/pronoun + have + Participle II

Will he have done? –Yes, he will / No, he won't
Shall we have gone by that time? – Yes, I think so.
Shall I have left before he comes? – No, you can stay, if you like.

They will have finished the exercise by the end of the lesson.

Will they have finished the exercise by the end of the lesson? –
Yes, they will.
Who will have finished the exercise by the end of the lesson? –
They will.
What will they have finished by the end of the lesson? – The
exercise.
When will they have finished the exercise? - By the end of the
lesson.
They will have finished the exercise by the end of the lesson,
won't they? – Yes, they will.

They will not have finished their discussion until you interfere.

Who will not have finished the discussion until you interfere? –
They won't.
Will they not have finished their discussion until you interfere? –
No, they won't.
Will they have finished their discussion or not until you interfere?
– They will not.
What will they have not finished? – Their discussion.
They will not have finished their discussion until you interfere,
will they? – No, they won't.
Until when they will not have finished their discussion? – Until
you interfere.

# Present Perfect Continuous

We use the present perfect continuous tense to show the action, which:

    1. started in the past

    2. was lasting for a certain period of time and

    3. continues at the moment of speaking.

We use the prepositions "for - в течение", "since – с, с тех пор, с тех пор как".

> Have (has) been + Participle I (Verb+ing)

I, we, you, they - Have been doing
He, she, it - Has been doing

Are you still learning French words, Tom? – Yes, I am.
How long <u>have</u> you <u>been learning</u> them?
I <u>have been learning</u> the words <u>for</u> an hour, but I still don't remember them.

Where is Jane? – She is in her room. She <u>has been writing</u> letters to her friends <u>since</u> breakfast.

Where is David? – He is in his study. He <u>has been reading</u> newspapers there since he came back from the office.

I've been learning English for two years. – So has Mary.

Clare has been watching TV since 5 o'clock. – So have I.

Действие началось в прошлом, длилось определенный период времени и продолжается в момент разговора.

    "since" / "for"

Ken is working for our company now. He has been working since last year.

Children are playing in the garden. They have been playing for half an hour.

Sue is attending Art Courses. She has been attending for three months.

I am reading a very interesting novel. I have been reading since 8 o'clock.
Don't go out. It is raining. It has been raining since early morning.
The director is having talks. He has been having talks for two hours.

Students are writing the test. They have been writing it for a long time.

Negative form:

| Noun / pronoun + have / has not been + Participle I |
| --- |

I, we, you, they – Have not been doing (haven't been)
He, she, it - Has not been doing (hasn't been)

I haven't been waiting for long.
He hasn't been waiting for long.
Don't worry, they haven't been waiting for you for long.
It hasn't been snowing either in the evening or in the morning.
I haven't been meeting the foreign delegation. – Neither has Tom.
Ann hasn't been dancing for long. - Neither have I.

Questions:

| 1. Have/has + noun / pronoun + been + participle I |
| --- |
| 2. Question word + have/has + noun/pronoun + been + participle I |

Have you been reading for the whole day? –
No, I haven't, just for an hour.

Has Liz been watching telly for long? – Yes, she has, since lunchtime.

Has Mr. Dunn been waiting for long? – He has been waiting for you since 10 o'clock. He is in the office now.

For how long have you been discussing the prices? – We've been discussing them for an hour.

Since when has she been dancing? – She started when a child of 4 years old.

## Past Perfect Continuous

The past perfect continuous tense shows an action that:
1. started in the past,
2. continued until another time in the past.

In this case we use "since, for, when + past indefinite"

> nouns / pronouns + had been + Participle I
> had been doing

Jack had been reading when I came.
He had been reading since he came from school.
He had been reading for two hours by that time.

Den had been working in the garden when I drove past their house.
He had been working since early morning.
He had been working for about three hours that day.

Janine had been ironing when her kids (children) appeared at the doorstep. (на пороге)

Negative sentence:

> Noun/ pronoun + had not been + Participle I

had not been = hadn't been

When I came, Jack had not been reading; he was fast asleep.

Den hadn't been working in the garden when I drove past their house; he had been talking to his wife.

Janine hadn't been ironing when her kids appeared at the doorstep; she had been washing the window at that time

Questions:

| |
| --- |
| 1. Have/has + noun / pronoun + been + participle I |
| 2. Question word + have/has + noun / pronoun + been + participle I |

Had Jack been reading when you came? – Yes, he had.

Had Den been working in the garage when you drove past their house? – No, he hadn't. He'd been working in the garden.

Had Janine been ironing when her kids went to school? – No, she had not. She had been ironing when her kids came from school.

Mr. Blake had been driving when the rain started.
Who had been driving when the rain started? - Mr. Blake had.
Had Mr. Blake been driving when the rain started? - Yes, he had.
Had Mr. Blake been driving when the rain stopped? – No, he hadn't.
Had Mr. Blake been driving when the rain started or stopped? –
When the rain started.
What had Mr. Blake been doing when the rain started? – He had been driving.
Mr. Blake had been driving when the rain started, hadn't he? –
Yes, he had.
Had Mr. Blake been driving or sitting next to the driver? -
Mr. Blake hadn't been sitting next to the driver.
He had been driving.

# Future Perfect Continuous

The Future Perfect Continuous tense shows an action that:
    1.  started and continued in the past,
    2.  is continuing now
    3.  will continue in the future and either
            a) may be completed by a certain time in the future
or
            b) may last longer

In this case we use "by, in, when + past indefinite"

| Noun / pronoun + will have been + Participle I (V+ing) |
| --- |

will have been doing = 'll have been doing

By next year, I will have been working for 40 years.
I hope we'll have been completing the construction next month.
In a year, I will have been graduating from the university.
I will have been driving far away from here in a couple of days.
I will have been sleeping when dad comes.
I will have been working for 50 years when I am retired.
I'll have been working for 50 years by the end of this year.
We'll have been finishing the test in 15 minutes.

Negative form:

| Noun/pronoun + will not (won't) have been + Participle I (V+ing) |
| --- |

I will not have been graduating from the university next year, I need two more years.
I won't have been sleeping when dad comes. I'll be waiting for him.
We'll not have been finishing the test in 15 minutes.

Questions:

| 1. Will + noun / pronoun have been + participle I |
| --- |
| 2. Question word+ will + noun/pronoun + have been + participle I |

Will you have been working for 40 years next year?

Will she have been graduating from the university in a year?
Will you have been working for 50 years by the end of the year?

The builders will have been accomplishing the construction by the first of September.

Who will have been accomplishing the construction by the first of September? – The builders will.

Will the builders have been accomplishing the construction by the first of September? – Yes, they will.

What will the builders have been accomplishing by the first of September? - The construction.

Will the builders have been accomplishing the construction by the first or by the 20th of September? – By the first of September.

By what date will the builders have been accomplishing the construction? - By the first of September.

The builders will have been accomplishing the construction by the first of September, won't they? – Yes, they will.

Do not try to use all tenses in one go. You will just mix them up. Do one at a time. First, practise well the first one; and only then gradually all the rest, in the range I've given to you.

# Modal verbs and Equivalents

In the first book, we have studied three base modal verbs and their main meanings:

Must –strong obligation
Can – ability
May – permission

We know, that modal verbs:
>   1. have no infinitive form,
>   2. have no "-s" ending with He, She, It,
>   3. the verbs following them are used without "to",
>   4. they do not need an auxiliary verb.

| All nouns/pronouns + modal verb + verb |
| --- |

Toni can sing opera arias. We can sing opera arias.
Toby may leave the lessons earlier. You may leave the lessons.
Gregory must join the army. Young men must join the army.

May we watch this film? - No, you must not. The film is not for children. You can take your ball and play football in the garden.

There is one more specific feature of the above modal verbs – some of them don't have past or future tenses.

To express their meaning in the past and in the future,
we use their Equivalents.

| Must – have to. Can – be able to. May – be allowed to. |
| --- |

Present – I must check. I can speak. I may go out.
I have to check. I am able to speak. I am allowed to go out.
Past – I had to check. I was able to speak. I was allowed to go out.
Future – I will have to check. I will be able to speak. I will be allowed to go out.

Negative sentences:

Present tense – I don't have to check.
Past tense – I wasn't able to speak.
Future tense – I won't be allowed to go out.

Questions:

Present tense – Do you have to check?
Past tense – Were you able to speak?
Future tense – Will you be allowed to go out?

The equivalents can be changed in all tenses according to the general grammar rules.

In English there are 8 verbs more and also two expressions, that behave like modals verbs:

Verbs – may, might, could, should, would, dare, let, ought to
Expressions – had better, need not (need to)

The modal verbs express the following functions:

Permission – Разрешение
Ability – Способность
Obligation – Обязательство
Prohibition – Запрет
Lack of necessity – Отсутствие необходимости
Advice – Консультация, совет
Possibility – Возможность
Probability – Вероятность

The expressions
had better = 'd better – лучше, лучше бы, было бы лучше
had better to – лучше бы
had better not – лучше не
had better or – лучше или
need not – не надо, не нужно = needn't
need not know – нет необходимости знать
need not worry – не нужно беспокоиться

**"could"** – past tense of "can"

1.  Ability in the past

When I was a child, I could play different sports games. I could not play chess (шахматы) and I couldn't jump off the garage roof. Could you jump off the garage roof?

2.  Polite permission – мог(ли) бы

Could you help me? = Не могли бы вы мне помочь?
Could I use your pen for a minute?
Could you open the door for me, please?

3.  Possibility – Take the umbrella, it could start raining.
    He could spend a month or two in the mountains.

"Could have done" – it was possible to happen but it didn't. (followed by perfect tense)

It was stupid of you to throw it out of the window, you <u>could have killed</u> someone. - Было глупо с твоей стороны выбросить это из окна, ты мог кого-нибудь убить.

**"would"**

1.  Past of "will"
I said I would help you. Я сказал, что помогу тебе.
I said I wouldn't help you. Я сказал, что не буду тебе помогать.
He told me he would be here before 8:00.
He told me he would not be here before 8:00.

2.  Repetition in past

When I was a kid, I would always go to the beach.
Когда я был ребенком, я бы всегда ходил на пляж.
When I was a kid, I wouldn't go into the water by myself.
В детстве я бы не пошел в воду один.
When he was young, he would always do his homework.
When he got older, he would never do his homework.

You can also change the first part of the sentences with "used to"

When I used to be a kid, I would always go to the beach.
When he used to be young, he would always do his homework.

3. Conditional clause – (бы)

I would buy it, if I had money. = Я бы это купил, если бы у меня были деньги.

Would she reduce the taxes, if she were president?

"I would like" = I'd like – я хотел бы, мне хотелось бы,
I would prefer – я бы предпочел

I'd like… - is a polite way to say "I want".
I am thirsty. I'd like a drink.
I'd like an orange, please. = Can I have an orange?

I'd like some information about hotels, please.
I'd like to watch the film on television this evening.

Would you like … ? – is a polite way to ask "Do you want?"

We use "Would you like … ?":

1. to offer things

Would you like some coffee? - No, thank you.
Would you like a bar of chocolate? – Yes, please.
What would you like, tea or coffee? – Tea, please.

*At the restaurant*:

- What would you like, madam?
- Not sure, anything for a starter.
- I would recommend you a fresh prawn salad.
- Thank you, but I would prefer a salad with cold chicken.
-

2. to invite somebody

Would you like to go for a walk? – Oh, yes, with great pleasure.

Would you like to have dinner with us on Sunday? – Yes, I'd love to. = I would like to have dinner with you.

What would you like to do this evening? – I'd like to watch a new comedy.

### Difference: **Would you like … ? Do you like…?**

Would you like … ? – Yes, I'd like… / No, I wouldn't. (now)
Do you like …? - Yes, I do. / No, I don't. (in general)

Would you like some tea? = Do you want some tea now?
Would you like to go to the cinema tonight? = Do you want to go to the cinema tonight? – Yes, I'd love to.
What would you like to do next weekend? – I would like to stay at home.

Do you like tea? – Yes, I do, but not very strong.
Do you like going to the cinema? - Yes, I go to the cinema a lot.
I like oranges. (in general) And you? Do you like them? - No, I don't, I prefer clementines.
What do you like to do at weekends? - I like spending time in the open air.

*Dialogues:* 1. Do you like tea? – Yes, I do.
Would you like some now? – No, thank you. Not now.

2. Do you like watching science fiction? – Oh, yes, very much.
Would you like to see a new one now? – That'll be lovely.

### "should"= "ought to"

It is a good thing to do, it is the right thing to do – следовало бы, должен.
But remember: "should" *and* "ought to" <u>are not</u> as strong as "must" and "have to".

Should be = ought to be – должно быть
Should have = ought to have – должен иметь
Should do = ought to do – должен сделать
It is a good film; we should go and see it. = we ought to go.

When you play tennis, you should always watch the ball. =
You always ought to watch the ball.

You should speak to him about it. = You ought to speak to him.
He should see a doctor. = He ought to see a doctor.
We should ask a lawyer. = We ought to ask a lawyer.

### Negative form of the sentences

should not do =  shouldn't do = it is not a good thing to do.

ought not to do - You ought not to do that!

You shouldn't make that mistake.
You ought not to make that mistake.

We shouldn't buy this sofa, it won't match our lounge.
You shouldn't rush to the doctor, take a painkiller (болеутоляющее).
I think they are too young. They ought not to get married so soon.

The negative and interrogative forms of 'ought to' are becoming
increasingly rare (все реже). We use "should" more often.

### Questions

What time should we arrive? – I think in an hour.
What are those children doing in the street? Shouldn't they be at
school?
Should you go to work now? You are not well this morning.
Do you think Patrick ought to work on Saturday? – Yes, I do. /
Yes, he ought to.  /  He needs to.  / Yes, he should.

  "Should" and "ought to" are basically the same,
although "should" is much more widely used than "ought to".

"Should" has less of a moral flavour.

You ought to tell her how you feel. - You cannot avoid telling her how you feel.

You should tell her how you feel. - It is better to tell her how you feel.

Both "should" and "ought to" are used to talk about:

1. obligation - You ought to stand back from the edge of the platform.
2. duty - You ought to vote in the coming election.
3. to give advice - You ought to have seen the film; it was very good.

You ought to arrive by noon if you take the motorway.

Followed by the perfect tense
Should have done / ought to have done

You should have tried the coat on before you bought it.
(this was a good idea but you didn't do it)

You shouldn't have bought a coat of this colour.
(this wasn't a good idea but you did it)

We ought to have booked in advance; there are no tickets left.

### "I think .... should"

I think it is a good idea. I think Dan should come to the classes.

We use "should *and* ought to":

1. For giving advice or a recommendation.

I think he should (ought to) resign now.
I think we should (ought to) invest more in Asia.
I think they should (ought to) do something about this terrible train service.

2. Obligation (weaker than "must / have to")

My buspass (проездной билет на автобус) is expired.
I should (ought to) apply for a new one.

Naine has got a terrible toothache, I think she should (ought to) go to the dentist.

We are short of bread, I think I should go shopping.

3. Logical conclusion

Tom goes to bed very late and he's always tired.
I think he should go to bed earlier. = Tom ought to go to bed earlier.

Questions with "I think"

| |
|---|
| 1. Do you think + noun/pronoun + should + verb + … |
| 2. Question word + do you think + noun/pronoun + should + verb |

Do you think I should buy this hat? – Yes, I think you ought to.
What time do you think we should go home? – We ought to go now.
Where do you think they went? – Should be to the bank.

"Ought" is the only form,
which has no past, no future, no modals in front of it.

You ought to be like your dad. You ought not to do that.

"should / ought to" with  the continuous

| |
|---|
| should + be + verb-ing |
| ought to + be + verb-ing |

Why are you watching TV? You should be working!
I think I should be leaving on business.
I think everybody ought to be listening to the news on TV or the radio.
I don't think you should be waiting for so long.

**"Should / Would"**- We use them if we want to express:

1. Past tense of "shall / will" (future in the past) – He was wondering how he would get to the station.

2. Subjunctive conditional, implying a negative – What would you do, if you had much money?

3. Duty or obligation (= ought to) – He should be home by now. You shouldn't eat peas with a knife.

4. A wish – I should (would) like you to play some Chopin for me. = I wish you would play.

5. A polite request – Would you shut the door, please?

*Compare*:  "Will you shut the door, please?" -
                     It's more polite than "Shut the door, please."


**"Might"**

It's the past of "may"

We use it tentatively (ориентировочно) to ask permission or to express a polite request.

Might – можно          Might do – можно сделать
Might be – возможно    Might not – может не
Might have – должно быть

Advise me of any hotel where I might spend a night.
Посоветуйте мне отель, где можно переночевать.

We use "Might" to express:

1. Polite permission / request

Might I offer my escort to you?
Might I give you an idea, which has just struck me?
Might you come to the exhibition with me?

The match might be postponed because of their request.
You might go out if your homework is ready.
The kids might be allowed to watch cartoons depending on their behaviour.

2. possibility, probability

I might come to you a bit sooner.

The train might be late.

We might catch the taxi to come there in time.

The office manager might have sent me there deliberately not to catch up with the boss.

The animals running from the forest might indicate some disaster.

In some years, we might find humans on other planets.

Our grandchildren might live longer, be stronger and be better developed.

Why are you crying? You might be lost.

### Negative sentences: Might not

I might not go to work tomorrow.
Sue might not come to the party.
You haven't kept your word; I might not trust you anymore.
Barny might not phone until he knows the result.

### The modal verbs followed by the perfect tense

| Noun/pronoun + modal verb + have + Participle II + | | | | |
|---|---|---|---|---|
| Children | might | have | broken | the glass. |

They might have got in through the window.
Они могли проникнуть через окно.

We could have broken the mirror. Мы могли разбить зеркало.

You should have spent more time learning the grammar.
Вам следовало потратить больше времени на изучение грамматики.

**"Let"** = allow – предлагать, позволить

We use the verb "let":

1. to offer to do something or to go somewhere

Let us – let's. Let's read it. – Давай почитаем это.
It's very hot; let's go to the lake. – Очень жарко; пойдем к озеру.
I am tired; let's have a break for a cup of coffee.

> Let + noun/pronoun + verb

2. to allow somebody to do something

Let Tom go. – Позвольте Тому уйти.
Please, let him go.

Samantha has let me in.

Don't stop her, let Ann try walking; she'll do that.

Let's go to the cinema, Jane. – I'd like to, but I think there'll be many people there. – Oh, no, there won't. Not on Monday.

So, will you ride the bike or not? – Let me think, I am not sure.

Could you let me talk to Linda? I think I'll be able to persuade her. Не могли бы вы позволить мне поговорить с Линдой? Думаю, мне удастся ее убедить.

Could you be so kind to let me know your decision as soon as possible? Не могли бы вы сообщить мне свое решение как можно скорее?

## "Dare" = сметь, посметь, пренебрегать опасностью

The verb has the forms:
dares – for "he, she, it" in positive sentences
daring – participle I
dared – in past negative sentences

We use the verb "dare"

1. To challenge a person to do something as proof of courage (доказательство смелости).

2. Something is done in response to such a challenge. (To oppose without fear - Противостоять без страха)

You only look at her! She dares argue with the general director.

I dare say, you are not right, Sir.

### Negative form – dare not = daren't

Steve dared not oppose his order. Dare you?
Стив не осмелился выступить против его приказа.

### Using "to" depends:

Dare you go there alone? – No, I daren't =
Do you dare **to** go there alone? – No, I don't
Осмелишься ли ты пойти туда одна?

How dare you talk to me like that? =
How can you dare **to** talk to me like that?
Как ты посмел так со мной разговаривать?

I don't even dare ask him for money. =
I don't even dare **to** ask him for money.
Я даже не смею просить у него денег.

He stood in front of his father, not daring to look into his eyes.
He stood in front of his father, daring not to look into his eyes.
Он стоял перед отцом, не смея смотреть ему в глаза.

## "Need (нужно)

The verb "need" works as an ordinary verb, according to the rules.

I need to go out. He needs to go out. We needed to go out.

I don't need to go. He doesn't need to go. We didn't need to go.

Do you need to go? Does he need to go? Did we need to go?

Negative – need not = "needn't"

**"needn't"** – lack of necessity – follows the rules of modal verbs.

*Compare*: I don't need to go. = I needn't go.
I need to talk. – есть "to" после "need"
I don't need to talk. – есть "to" после "don't need"
I needn't talk - нет "to" после "needn't"

needn't do (no "to") - needn't speak, needn't fly

You needn't open your suitcase. She needn't do that either.

They needn't go to the factory. We needn't go there either.

I have a shower every day. – Must you do it every day? –
No, I needn't, but I like to.

Mr. Kirk needn't check all the accounts, but he thought it would be more reliable.

My mother needn't meet me after my lessons, she was just overcaring.

### "Had better"

Had better = 'd better – лучше, лучше бы, было бы лучше

We use "had better" to give stronger advice, especially when there could be a negative consequence if the advice is ignored.

You'd better ask for his forgiveness.
Вам лучше попросить у него прощения.
You'd better call the doctor.
You'd better have a good rest.
You had better not be late.
You'd better not leave your key in the door.
You'd better not promise, to be on the safe side.
На всякий случай лучше не обещать.

## "be, do, have"

1. Notional verbs

As notional verbs, they have semantic meaning in the sentence and are translated:

**"be"** – быть, являться, находиться

Present simple - Be – am, is, are – semantic verb (semantic verb)
I am a teacher. He is clever. She is beautiful. We are here

Past simple - Be - was, were - I was a teacher. He was clever.
She was beautiful. We were here. Were they here?

Future simple – I shall be a teacher. He will be clever.
She will be beautiful. We shall be here. Will they be here?

**"do"** – делать, выполнять

Present indefinite – I do many things at work. He does his task.
She does her exercise. They do their job.

Past indefinite – I did many things at work. He did his task.
She did her exercise. They did their job.

Future Indefinite - I shall do many things at work. He will do his task. She will do her exercise. They will do their job.

**"have"** – иметь

Present indefinite – I have a house. He has his flat. They have a job.

Past indefinite – I had a house. He had his flat. They had a job.

Future Indefinite - I shall have a house. He will have a flat.
They will have a nice job.

Also the verb **"have"** has the following meanings:

a) Have got (standard expression). = Have – I've got a pen.
b) Have to do = (modal equivalent) must do – I have to go.
He has to go.
c) Auxiliary verb in Perfect tense. I have spent all money.
She has forgotten. He had lost his temper before she realised that.

### 2. Auxiliary verbs, forming grammar tenses

As auxiliary verbs, they create grammar tenses, negative
sentences and questions.

**"be"**- points to the continuous tense.

Present continuous – Be (am, is, are) + Verb-ing

I am working now. It isn't raining at the moment.
What are you doing this evening?

Past continuous - Be (was, were) + Verb-ing

I was working when she arrived. It wasn't raining, so we went
out. What were you doing at 3 o'clock?

Future continuous – Will / Shall + Be + Verb-ing

I shall be working for the whole day. It won't be raining, so we
can go out. What will you be doing at 3 o'clock?

**"do"** – indicates the indefinite tense.

Present indefinite – "do / does" only in negative sentences and
questions.
I work every day. I don't work on Sunday. Do you work?

Past indefinite – "did" only in negative sentences and questions.
I worked last year. I didn't work yesterday. Did he work?

**"have"** – forms the perfect tense.

Present perfect - have, has + past participle

I have cleaned them. Barbara hasn't clean them.
Tom has lost his passport. Where have Paul and Linda gone?

Past perfect – had + past participle (participle II)

I had cleaned my room before they arrived.
Tom had lost his passport, that's why he couldn't get through the customs.
The policeman came after they had gone.

Future Perfect - will have + Participle II

I will have cleaned my room by 2 o'clock.
He will have done the task before the end of the lesson.
They will have built it by May.

### 3. Auxiliary verb "Be", forming passive voice

Present passive - be (am, is, are) + participle II: The room is cleaned.

Past passive – be (was, were) + participle II: The room was cleaned.

Future passive – will be + participle II: The room will be cleaned.

We shall be studying the passive voice a bit further in this book

So: the verbs "be, do, have" as auxiliary, present grammar tenses.

"be" – continuous tenses; also forms the passive voice

"do" – indefinite tenses

"have" – perfect tenses

# Infinitive

There are three forms of the verb: Infinitive, Participle I and Participle II.

**The Infinitive** is the base form of a verb.

The present infinitive has two forms:
   a)  "to"+ base = "to-infinitive": to drop, to work, to do, to walk
   b)  infinitive with no "to", called "zero infinitive": drop, work, do, walk

1.     "Zero infinitive" is the simple form of the verb that you can find in the dictionaries.

"Zero infinitive" functions in the sentence as a verb in the meaning of a predicate (сказуемое), showing an action.

I <u>want</u> to help you. - Я хочу помочь тебе.
"want – хочу" is a predicate.

I <u>need</u> to go. - Мне надо идти.
"need – надо- нуждаюсь" is a predicate.

<u>Take</u> the rubbish to put it in the bin.
<u>Возьми</u> мусор, чтобы выбросить его в мусорный ящик.
"take – возьми" is also a predicate.

We use "zero infinitive" after the following verbs:
feel, hear, help, let, make, see, watch.

I heard my naughty kitten mew under my bed.
"heard" is a predicate.
"my naughty kitten" is an object.
"mew: is a "zero infinitive".

In this sentence, the verb "hear" is followed by a direct object and then "zero infinitive".

My friend helped me understand that task.
You made me jump. = You scared me. Ты напугал меня
Let us think first. Давайте сначала подумаем.
I watched her make the cake. Я смотрел, как она готовила торт.

2.      To-infinitive does not function as a predicate in a sentence.

To-infinitive can function as an attribute (определение), an
object (дополнение) or adverbials (обстоятельства).

Take the rubbish to put it in the bin.
What rubbish? – which should be put in the bin.
"to put it in the bin" is an attribute.

I bought this fabric to make a new dress.
Bought why? - to make a new dress.
"to make a new dress" is an adverbial of reason.

I want to help you.
I want what? – to help.
"to help – помочь" is an object.

We went to the field to see how the crops grow.
Went what for? - to see how the crops grow
"to see how the crops grow" is an adverbial of purpose.

The art gallery has teamed up with local artists to organize
an outdoor exhibition in the park.

Художественная галерея объединилась с местными
художниками, чтобы организовать выставку под открытым
небом в парке.

The Infinitive can be:

### 1. Active Infinitive

He asked the student on duty to open the window.
She watched the children play in the garden.

### 2. Passive Infinitive

He ordered the window to be shut.
This work must be done in three days.

### 3. Continuous Infinitive

It is pleasant to be swimming in the warm water.
They must be walking in the garden now.

### 4. Perfect Infinitive

I am pleased to have met him yesterday
She was absent yesterday, she may have been ill.

## The Infinitive Constructions

### 1. Objective with the Infinitive

I want you to come earlier.
I saw him cross the street.

### 2. For – Construction

It is difficult for me to do this task.
The text is easy enough for you to understand.

### 3. Nominative with the Infinitive

They were asked to come earlier.
He is sure to come soon.

# Participle

There are two forms of the participle in English.

English verbs have the present participle (Participle I) and the past participle (Participle II)

Participle I and Participle II have some qualities of verbs.

We use them: in the formation of the continuous and perfect tenses (he is writing, he has written); in the creation of passive voice (the letter is being written, the letter has been written). They can function as an adjective as well (breaking news, broken leg).

English participles are translated into Russian as verbs, adjectives, participles (причастий) and adverbial participles (деепричастий).

The simple forms of participles (for example: participle I - writing, participle II - written) are used in the formation of tenses.

It's the main function of the participles.

When the participle becomes a part of the tense form, with the auxiliary verb, then it is a part of a sentence, not a participle.

They <u>are painting</u>. – The present continuous tense. – Они красят.

They <u>have painted</u>. – The present perfect tense. – Они покрасили.

# The Present Participle
## (Participle I)

Verb + "-ing" ending – live – living, work – working.

It is an exciting story. Это захватывающая история.

He was sitting in an armchair watching TV.
Он сидел в кресле и смотрел телевизор.

There was a lot of snow lying on the ground.
На земле лежало много снега.

When I entered the room, they stopped talking.
Когда я вошел в комнату, они перестали разговаривать.

Be careful at the street crossing.
Будьте осторожны на переходе.

When crossing the street be attentive.
При переходе улицы будьте внимательны.

Watching boats going up and down the river, he dreamed about his future.
Наблюдая за лодками, плывущими по реке, он мечтал о своем будущем.

The present participle can replace any active tense:

a) The people crossing the road must be careful.
The people, who cross the road, must be careful.

b) Do I know the man looking at you?
Do I know the man, who is looking at you?

c) The elderly woman sitting here last week used to be a famous actress. The elderly woman, who sat here last week, used to be a famous actress.

Participle I can be used:

1.      as a verb in the sentence in the present, past, future and perfect continuous tense:

a) A fragile girl is dancing on the stage.
На сцене танцует хрупкая девушка.

The present continuous tense.

A fragile girl was dancing on the stage yesterday.
The past continuous tense.

I hope this fragile girl will be dancing on the stage of Paris.
The future continuous tense.

The girl has been dancing since her early childhood.
The present perfect continuous tense.

By the end of the performance, the girl will have been dancing for two hours.

b) A young couple is walking along the alley.
По аллее гуляет молодая пара.

c) The man was shaking my hand quite friendly.
Мужчина довольно дружелюбно пожимал мне руку.

2.   as an adjective:

a) The dancing girl looked so fragile. Танцующая девушка выглядела такой хрупкой. "dancing" is the adjective, characterising the noun "girl". What girl? - Dancing girl.

b) The walking young couple reminded me of my youth.
Гуляющая молодая пара напомнила мне мою молодость.
"walking" is the adjective, describing the noun "couple"

c) Shaking my hand, the man seemed to be friendly.
Пожимающий мне руку мужчина казался мне дружелюбным.
Which man? The one, who was shaking my hand.

3. as an active participial clause:

a) The girl, dancing on the stage, looked so fragile.
Девушка, танцующая на сцене, выглядела такой хрупкой. =

The girl, who danced on the stage, looked so fragile.
Девушка, которая танцевала на сцене, выглядела такой хрупкой.

b) The young couple, walking along the alley, reminded me of my youth. Молодая пара, гулявшая по аллее, напомнила мне мою молодость. =
The young couple, that walked along the alley, reminded me my youth. Молодая пара, которая гуляла по аллее, напомнила мне мою молодость.

c) The man, shaking my hand, looked straight into my eyes.
Мужчина, пожимая мне руку, посмотрел мне прямо в глаза. =

The man, who was shaking hands, looked straight into my eyes.
Мужчина, который обменивался рукопожатием, смотрел мне прямо в глаза.

4. in the function of adverbials:

a) The girl danced on the stage, smiling at the audience.
Девушка танцевала на сцене, улыбаясь публике.
Danced how? – Smiling.

b) The young couple, who reminded me of my youth, was walking along the alley.
Молодая пара, напомнившая мне мою молодость, шла по аллее.
Was walking where? - Along the alley.

c) He shook my hand looking straight into my eyes.
Он пожал мне руку, глядя мне прямо в глаза.
Shook how? – Looking into my eyes.

## The Present Participle Constructions

The objective with the Present Participle - I see them <u>crossing</u> the street. I heard somebody walking in the hall.
A minute later, she found all the children swimming in the pond.
The old woman watched the children playing in the garden.

## The Functions of the Participle I

### 1. Attribute - определение

They watched the rising sun from the balcony of the hotel
The man sitting opposite the window was a famous doctor
There is no time left for having fun.

### 2. Adverbial – обстоятельственный (наречие – how?)

When leaving don't forget to shut all the windows.
Saying that he left the room.
They spent a week there visiting art galleries and museums.

## The present participle with complex object

Usually, it is used after the verbs of sense "feel, hear, notice, observe, see and watch". It indicates the action in progress.

I saw Sue knocking on the door.
Sue felt me looking at her.
She heard somebody coming up to the door.
Sue looked back noticing me watching her.
The door opened and I switched my attention, observing the woman, who eyed Sue.
"Oh, my God!" – the woman cried out, they both smiled.
I observed the scene, anticipating me writing a new novel.

# The Past Participle

## (Participle II)

Verb + "-ed" ending – live – lived, work – worked.

Participle II has some qualities of a verb and can participate in the formation of the perfect tenses, can create the passive voice and can be used as an adjective.

Very important to remember that English verbs are divided into regular and irregular.

The regular verbs have "-ed" ending, which is pronounced differently:

1. In the verbs with "y"ending – try, study, copy – we change "y" into "i" and add "-ed": try – tried, study – studied, copy – copied.

2. In the verbs, where the last letter (sound) is consonant – stop, plan, we double this consonant: stop – stopped, plan – planned.

3. The "-ed" ending after voiced consonants [b, g, v, z] and sonorous consonants are pronounced [d]: absorb – absorbed, boil – boiled, infer – inferred

4. The "-ed" ending after voiceless consonants [p, k, s, ʃ, tʃ] is pronounced [t]: push – pushed, stop – stopped, pick – picked, punch – punched.

5. "-ed" after last sounds [d, t] is read [id]: elect – elected, avoid – avoided, rotate – rotated, create – created.

The irregular verbs have their own form of participle II.
You can see them in the 4<sup>th</sup> column of the table with the irregular verbs (book one).

*Let's compare* the participle II

    1.  as a verb and as an adjective:

Past Indefinite - The teacher recommended us to read this book. (verb)

Past Participle - You can get the book recommended by the teacher in the library. (adjective)

He addressed his greetings to the delegation.
There is a letter addressed to your secretary.

The programme included many interesting places to see.
All the points included in the plan were discussed.

The lecturer answered all the interesting questions.
The questions answered by the lecturer were very interesting.

    2.  as perfect tenses and passive voice

This seat next to mine hasn't been taken. (passive voice)
Tony has taken this seat immediately. (perfect tense)

We have illustrated many magazines in our reading room.
Our magazines were illustrated in a classic manner.

I met friends on my way home.
My friends were met on my way home.

The football match has been watched by thousands of people.
Thousands of people have watched the football match.

Tom had taken a book from the shelf and sat down to read it.
Tom sat down to read the book, which had been taken from the shelf.

## Constructions with the Past Participle

The conference held in London was on the problems of economic development of the countryside of Sussex.

The committee had all the necessary documents prepared before the first sitting.

Watches and cameras made in Japan are very popular in all the countries.

The delegation answered all the questions asked by foreign correspondents.

They watched the meeting held in the central square of the town. The British delegation met by the committee representatives approached the Government House.

You will have an article for the newspaper written by the secretary.

## Objective construction with the Past Participle

I want my hair cut.
Where did you have your coat made?
Susan, go to your mother and have your face washed.
I want all the exercises done by tomorrow morning.
He left the room seen by no one.
Coming home, she found all rooms cleaned.

# Passive Voice

We use the passive voice when we are more interested in the action than in the person, who does the action.

It is not the object that performs the action; something happens to the object.

*Compare:* I push. Я толкаю. – active voice
I am pushed. – Меня толкают. - passive voice

In the first sentence, "I" is the subject.
In the second sentence, "I" is the object.

People speak English all over the world. – active voice
English is spoken all over the world. – passive voice

| Noun/pronoun + Be (in persons) + participle II + | | | |
|---|---|---|---|
| The dog | is | brushed | every week. |
| Собаку | | расчесывают | каждую неделю. |

## Present Passive Voice

I clean the office every day. (I do it) - Active voice.

The office is cleaned every day by me. (is done) - Passive Voice.

The desks are cleaned every morning.
Shops are closed at 4 pm.
I am thanked for everything.
English is spoken all over the world.
I am never invited to parties.
Butter is made from milk.
Oranges are imported into Britain.

Passive voice + "by":

Is done / made by somebody / something

This novel is written <u>by Collins</u>.
These plays are written <u>by Shakespeare.</u>
The dishes are washed by my mother.

Passive voice + "with":

Is done / made with something

The hands are washed with soap.
The dishes are washed with washing-up liquid.
The cake is sweetened with honey.

Passive voice + "in":

The letter is written in (with) pencil.
The wall is painted in blue colour.
The book is published in black and white.

Negative sentences:

| Noun/pronoun + | be (in persons) + | not + | participle II + | |
|---|---|---|---|---|
| The letters | are | not | taken | out. |

The novel is not written <u>by Collins</u>.
The hands are not washed by soap.
The letter is not written in pencil.

Questions:

| Question word + be (in persons) + noun/pronoun + participle II |
|---|
How often <u>are</u> these rooms <u>cleaned</u>? – They <u>are cleaned</u> daily.

<u>I have read a catching novel "Gone with the Wind".</u>
Who has read a catching novel "Gone with the Wind"? – I have.
Is the novel called "Gone with the Water"? – No, it isn't.
Is the novel called "Gone with the Sand"? – No, it isn't.
How is the novel called? – It's called "Gone with the Wind".
Who is the novel written by? – It is written by Margaret Mitchel.

# Past Passive Voice

Something happened to the object in the past.

| Noun/pronoun + was/were + Participle II + … | | | |
|---|---|---|---|
| The cat | was | given | some milk. |
| Кошке | | дали | молока. |

*Compare.* Many people from the town visited the seaside.
The seaside was visited by many people from the town.

He put the magazine into the bag. –
The magazine was put into the bag by him.

Today the lesson was given by a new teacher in a large hall.
We were woken up by a loud noise.
My brother was bitten by a dog last week.

Negative form:

| Noun/pronoun + was not/were not + Participle II + … |
|---|

The office was not cleaned yesterday.
This house wasn't built 100 years ago.
These houses were not built 100 years ago.
We weren't invited to the party last week.

The leaves weren't swept by the wind; they were swept by
the caretaker (лицо, присматривающее за домом).

Questions:

| 1. Was/were + noun/pronoun + Participle II + … |
|---|
| 2. Question word + Was/were + noun + Participle II |

1.

Tom was knocked down by a car, it was a terrible accident.
Тома сбила машина, это была ужасная авария.

Was Tom seriously injured? –
Yes, his right arm and leg were broken.
Was anybody else injured in the accident? –
Yes, two people were taken to the hospital.


2.

I <u>was born</u> in 1962. When <u>were you</u> born? –

I was born in Hastings. Where were you born? –

<u>The letter was written by Elizabeth to her aunt.</u>
Was the letter written by her? – Yes, it was.
Who was the letter written by? – By Elizabeth.
Who was the letter written to? – To her aunt.
The letter was written by Elizabeth, wasn't it? –Yes, it was.

<u>The telephone was invented by Alexander Bell.</u>
Was the telephone invented by Alexander Bell? – Yes, it was.
Who was the telephone invented by? – By Alexander Bell.
When was the telephone invented? – In February 1876
The telephone was invented by Alexander Bell, wasn't it? – Yes,
it was.

<u>Yesterday all the dishes were thoroughly cleaned with special</u>
<u>liquid by Ann.</u>
Yesterday all the dishes were thoroughly cleaned with special
liquid by Ann, weren't they? – Yes, they were.
When were all the dishes thoroughly cleaned? – Yesterday.
Were all the dishes thoroughly cleaned? – Yes, all of them were.
What was thoroughly cleaned by Ann? – All the dishes.
How were the dishes cleaned? – They were cleaned thoroughly.
What were the dishes cleaned with? – With special liquid.
Who were dishes cleaned by? – By Ann.

# Future Passive Voice

Positive sentence:

| Noun/pronoun + will be + Past participle + … | | | |
|---|---|---|---|
| She | will be | told | which bus to catch. |

The report will be prepared tomorrow.
The car will be cleaned before we make the trip.
Some modern music <u>will be played</u> by this orchestra.
The children will now be brought to school by bus.
This film will be remembered for a long time.
The question will be discussed later.

Negative sentence:

| Noun/pronoun + will not be (won't be) + Past participle + … | | | |
|---|---|---|---|
| She | won't be | told | what to do. |

The building will not be decorated in the winter.
There won't be ten competitors in the race.
The bedroom won't be cleaned by me today.
The teacher's correction won't be made in black.
Hurry up, they won't be kept waiting.

Questions:

| Question word + will + noun + be + Participle II + … | | | | | |
|---|---|---|---|---|---|
| When | will | she | be | told | what to do? |

Who will the part of Othello be sung by? – By William.
Who will a new song be written for this singer by? – By a famous composer.
Where will the children be taken by their parents on holiday? – To the South.
What day will the appointment be made for? - For Monday.
When will the interview be given? - In some minutes.

# Present Continuous Passive

Something is happening to an object at the present moment.

Positive sentence:

| Noun/pronoun + be (in persons) + being + Participle II + | | | |
|---|---|---|---|
| The door | is | being | repaired now. |
| Дверь | | | ремонтируют. |

*Compare:*
Somebody is painting the door. – The door is being painted

My car is being repaired. (somebody is repairing it)

Some new houses are being built opposite the park. (somebody is building them)

No matches are being played next Saturday. (there won't be any matches)

Negative sentences:

| Noun + is not/are not + being + Participle II + |
|---|

The office is not being cleaned at the moment.
The shirts are not being ironed now.
The car is not being repaired in the garage.
The windows are not being painted by me.
The trees are not being cut down.

Questions:

| Question word + is/are + being + Participle II + |
|---|

My car is being repaired at the garage by a good technician.
What is being repaired? - My car is.
Where is my car being repaired? - At the garage.
Who is my car being repaired by? - By a good technician.
Why is my car being repaired? – Because it was damaged.
My car is being repaired, isn't it? – Yes, it is.

Some new houses are being built opposite the park this year.
What is being built opposite the park this year? - Some new houses are.
Are some new houses being built this year? – Yes, they are.
Where are some new houses being built? – Opposite the park.
When are some new houses being built? – This year.
Some new houses are being built opposite the park this year, aren't they? - Yes, they are.

## Present Perfect Passive

Something happened to an object.

Positive sentence:

| Noun/pronoun + have been / has been + Participle II + ... | | | |
|---|---|---|---|
| The door | has | been | repaired by now. |
| Дверь | | | отремонтирована уже. |

We use the words: just, already, yet

Somebody <u>has painted</u> the bench. – The bench <u>has been painted</u>.
My car has been painted. (somebody has painted it)
My credit cards have been stolen. (somebody has stolen them)

The mistakes have just been corrected by our teacher.
The dishes have already been washed by my mother.
The address has been written correctly in black block letters.
The children have already been invited to see a new film.

Negative sentences:

| Noun + have not / has not + been + Participle II |
|---|

We often use the word "yet" (еще, до сих пор, однако).

The room has not been dusted yet.

I haven't been invited to the party.
Fresh apples have not been brought from the shop.
The chairs haven't been taken away to another room.
The work hasn't been done yet.

Questions:

| 1. Have / has + noun + been + Participle II |
| 2. Question word + have / has + noun + been + Participle II |

Has the shirt been washed? (has somebody washed it?)

Her hat has been blown off by the wind.
Has her hat been blown off by the wind? – Yes, it has.
What has been blown off? – Her hat.
What has her hat been blown off by? - By the wind.

Our new curtains have been bought by my mother the other day.
Who have our new curtains been bought by? – By my mother.
What has been bought by mother? - Our new curtains have.
When have our new curtains been bought? – The other day.
Our new curtains have been bought by mother, haven't they? –
Yes, they have.

# Gerund

Stop talking! I am sorry for coming late.
Do you mind my opening the window?
We agreed to Ann's going to the country.
He is interested in collecting stamps.

Attention! *Differentiate.*

Gerund - When a boy he was fond of reading books about adventures.

Noun - The reading of the article took him only a few minutes.

Verb - He is reading a very interesting book about adventures.

The functions of the Gerund.

1. Swimming is a good exercise. – Subject
2. Her greatest pleasure is reading. – Predicate
3. We think of going to the South in the summer. – Object
4. There are different ways of doing that. – Attribute
5. On coming home, he rang me up. – Adverbial

The Gerundial construction

Excuse my coming so late.
There is no hope of his getting the tickets.
We are interested in your taking part in the expedition.
There is no excuse for his doing such a thing.

Gerund and Infinitive

After some verbs, only the gerund is used, after others only the infinitive, and after some verbs, you can use either.

1. verbs followed by the gerund: avoid, dislike, enjoy, finish, mind (= object to)

2. verbs followed by the infinitive:

    a)        all the special verbs: can, may, must, ought, shall, will, let, used to, have

    b)        expect, hope, mean (= intend), promise, want and certain others

3. verbs followed by the gerund or the infinitive (begin, hate, learn, like, prefer, stop, forget, remember, see, hear, etc)

*Mind the difference:*

Present participle – verbal adjective: (dancing girl – the girl who dances). The dancing girl was very graceful. (изящный)

Verb (past continuous) – The girls were dancing gracefully.

Adjective – The doing a crossword boy is my brother.
Noun – Doing crosswords is his hobby.

Gerund – verbal noun (dancing-teacher – the person who teaches to dance)
The dancing-teacher was showing the correct position.

Object - Suzanne is interested in watching detective films.
Noun – Watching detective films is her favourite time.

# Future in the past

The Future in the past denotes future actions, planned or thought of in the past.
The Future in the past обозначает будущие действия, которые были запланированы или продуманы в прошлом.

We decided that you would enter the university.
Мы решили, что вы будете поступать в университет.

We usually use the Future in the past for the sequence of tenses and in the reported (indirect) speech.
Обычно мы используем the Future in the past при согласовании времён и в косвенной речи.

Let's work it out on the example of the sentence:
I thought that I would go. Я думал, что пойду.

In Russian, we say: Я думал, что пойду.
Я думал – past tense;    пойду – future tense.

The direct translation from Russian into English –
I thought that I will go. – It is not correct.

In English, there is a law of sequence of tenses (согласование времён). It means that we must use the whole sentence in the same tense.

What we do is:
We transform the auxiliary verb of the future tense "will" into "would" (past tense of "will").
I thought that I would go. – It is correct.
Now both parts of the sentence are in the past tense.

I never thought you would have won the match.
Никогда не думал, что вы выиграете матч.
He said that he would come. Он сказал, что приедет.

We use the Future in the past to express the thoughts in the past time about the future.

# Future Simple in the past

The simple tense has no actions, just the description of the subject: state – location, position, status, situation, etc.

The verb "be" is notional in this tense.

I am British. I am at work. I am married. I am happy.

The auxiliary verb "will", pointing to the future tense, turns into "would" – past tense of "will".

would be – I would be = I'd be  /  He would be = He'd be
         I said I would be with you. = I said I'd be with you.

*Let's compare*: I <u>am </u>here. – be + here – present simple
         I <u>will be</u> here. – future simple
         I <u>would be</u> here – future simple in the past –
         I promised I would be here.

Future simple: I will be at work tomorrow.
Future simple in the past: I would be at work the next day.

*What we have to transfer* Future simple *into* Future simple in the past:  1. will → would
         2. tomorrow → the next day

I thought I would be at work the next day.
Я думал, что на следующий день буду на работе.

      I thought <u>in the past about</u> my action in <u>the future.</u>

We use "the future simple in the past" in complex sentences.

| Complex sentence = main clause + subordinate clause |
| --- |

I thought – Main clause (главное предложение)

| Main clause = subject (noun/pronoun) + predicate (verb in the past) |
| --- |

We can use: I thought, she decided, we insisted, you dreamed, they said, etc.

I would be at work the next day. – Subordinate clause
(придаточное предложение)

Subordinate clause = subject (noun/pronoun) + would be + …

I felt very cold and I guessed that <u>I would be ill the next day.</u>

Positive sentence:

Main clause (in the past) + noun/pronoun + would be +…

I told you they <u>would be</u> in time. Я сказал вам, что они успеют.
I thought <u>we would</u> be very tired. Я думал, мы очень устанем.
The passengers knew that the train <u>would be</u> late.
Nadine <u>thought</u> with sadness that <u>next year</u> she <u>would be</u> 75.

Negative form:

In the subordinate clause we add "not" after "would"
would not = wouldn't = 'd not

Main clause + noun/pronoun + would not + be + …

He said he <u>would not be</u> glad to see them.=
He said he <u>wouldn't be</u> glad to see them. =
He said he<u>'d not be</u> glad to see them.
Он сказал, что не обрадуется их встрече.

Questions:

"I thought I would be at work." is a complex sentence
(сложноподчиненное предложение).

I thought – the main clause – основное (главное) предложение;
I would be at work. – the subordinate clause (придаточное
дополнительное предложение)

Example: He said that he would be glad to see them.

We ask the question only to the main clause (the main part of the
sentence) – "He said," – Did he say?

The subordinate clause – "he would be glad to see them." (придаточное предложение) is not changed. We just add it to the question.

---

Did he say + he would be glad to see them?

---

Now the question is: Did he say he would be glad to see them?

---

Questions:
a) Did + noun/pronoun + verb + subordinate clause
b) Question word + did + noun + verb

---

Did he say he would be glad to see them? – Yes, he did.
What did he say? – That he would be glad to see them.

Sandra said that the next day she would be at the exam.
Did Sandra say that the next day she would be at the exam? – Yes, she did.
What did Sandra say? – That the next day she would be at the exam.

### Future Indefinite in the past

The indefinite tense has actions that happen in our everyday life.

The future indefinite tense – I will go to work.

The future indefinite in the past tense – I decided that I would go to work.

The sentence in "the future indefinite in the past" is a complex sentence (main clause + subordinate clause).

The main clause (past tense) – I decided
The subordinate clause (future in the past) – I would go to work.

"will" → "would" - I decided I would go to work.

We use the first form of verbs (infinitive without "to") after "would"; the same as after "will".

would go, would sleep, would watch

would = 'd  -  I'd go, he'd sleep, they'd watch

### Positive sentence

They thought they would meet the following week.
They thought – main clause
they would meet the following week – subordinate clause

| Main clause + nouns/pronouns + would + verb + … |
|---|

They thought + they'd meet the following week.

We hoped she would take part in the concert.
We hoped she'd take part in the concert.

### Negative sentence:

In the subordinate clause we add "not" after "would"

We hoped she <u>would not</u> take part in the concert.

| Main clause + nouns/pronouns + would not + verb + … |
|---|

Would not = wouldn't = 'd not

I said I would not go to the doctor. =
I said I wouldn't go to the doctor. =
I said I'd not go to the doctor.

### We can add the word "rather" after "I'd"

I said I'd rather not go to the doctor.
Я сказал, что лучше не пойду к врачу.

She knew she wouldn't come back by 7 o'clock.
He wrote that he'd not go on the excursion.
They decided Mark wouldn't participate in the competition.

Questions

We ask the questions to the main clause.

a) Did + noun/ pronoun + verb + subordinate clause
b) Question word + did + noun/ pronoun + verb

Did they decide Mark wouldn't participate in the competition? –
Yes, they did.
What did they decide? – Mark wouldn't participate in the
competition.

Attention! Question "who?"

Just put the question word "who" instead of the subject.

Who hoped she <u>would not</u> take part in the concert? – We did.
Who decided Mark wouldn't participate in the competition? –
They did.

<u>Yesterday Tom thought he would take the kids to the park.</u>
Who thought that he would take the kids to the park? – Tom did.
Did yesterday Tom think he would take the kids to the park? –
Yes, he did.
What did Tom think yesterday? – He would take the kids to the
park.
When did Tom think that he would take the kids to the park? –
Yesterday.
Yesterday Tom thought that he would take the kids to the park,
didn't he? – Yes, Tom did. = Yes, he did.

<u>Sandra was afraid that the next day she would fail the exam.</u>
Who was afraid that the next day she would fail the exam? –
Sandra was.
Was Sandra afraid that the next day she would fail the exam? –
Yes, she was.
What was Sandra afraid of? – That the next day she would fail the
exam.

# Future Continuous in the Past

The continuous tense shows that actions take place at a certain time.

$$\boxed{\text{be} + \text{verb} + \text{"ing" ending}}$$

The present continuous – I am working now.

The future continuous – I will be working at 5 pm.

"will" → "would"

The future continuous in the past – I said I would be working at 5.

The construction of the future continuous in the past is:

Main clause (past tense) - noun /pronoun + verb in the past

Subordinate clause - noun /pronoun + would be + verb-ing

After "would" we use the verb "be" + participle I

would be going, would be sleeping, would be watching

would = 'd – I'd be going, he'd be sleeping, they'd be watching

"Dad said"- the main clause
"he would be working till late." - subordinate clause

Dad said that he would be working till late.
Dad said that he'd be working till late.

Positive sentence

Main clause + subordinate clause (would be v-ing)

The passengers knew that the train would be arriving later.

I thought we would be working the next day. =
I thought we'd be working the next day.

We hoped she would be taking part in the evening concert.
= We hoped she'd be taking part in the evening concert.

Negative sentence: "would not" + "be v-ing"

I said I <u>would not be going</u> to the doctor.

---

| Main clause + subordinate clause (would not be v-ing) |
| --- |

Would not = wouldn't = 'd not

I said I would not be going to the doctor.
I said I wouldn't be going to the doctor.
I said I'd not be going to the doctor.

He wrote that he would not be going on the excursion.
He wrote that he wouldn't be going on the excursion.
He wrote that he'd not be going on the excursion.

The managers decided that they <u>wouldn't be speaking</u> to the staff until the director's approval.

### Questions

We ask the questions to the main clause adding the subordinate clause with no changes.

---

a) Did + noun/ pronoun + verb + subordinate clause
b) Question word + did + noun/ pronoun + verb

---

<u>The staff demanded that they would come to work at 8.30.</u>
Who demanded that they would come to work at 8.30? – The staff did.
Did the staff demand that they would come to work 8.30? – Yes, they did

What did the staff demand? – They demanded that they would come to work at 8.30.

The children were excited that they would be going to the zoo on Sunday.

Who was excited that they would be going to the zoo on Sunday? – The children were.

Were the children excited that they would be going to the zoo on Sunday? – Yes, they were.

Why were the children excited? – Because they would be going to the zoo on Sunday.

### Future Perfect in the Past

The perfect tense is formed by: have + participle II

We have worked it out. I have done it.

1. The future perfect:

| Any noun/pronoun + will have + participle II + (by) +... |
| --- |

We shall have worked it out. I will have done it.

2. The future perfect in the past:

| Any noun/pronoun + would have + participle II + (by) +... |
| --- |

He assured they would have completed it by the following Saturday.
Он заверил, что они завершат его к следующей субботе.

In the future perfect in the past we use complex sentences:

The main clause – past tense – "He assured"

The subordinate clause – future perfect in the past – "they would have completed it by the following Saturday"

> Main clause (past tense) + subordinate clause (future perfect in the past)

I thought + we would have finished this work by 2.
He said he would have finished this work by 2.

I dreamed how I would have knocked Tom out.
Приснилось, как я нокаутировал Тома .

They hoped we would have reached the peak of the rock.
Они надеялись, что мы достигнем вершины скалы.

Sam didn't even dream she would have married such a man.
Сэм даже не мечтала, что выйдет замуж за такого человека.

### Negative sentence: would not

> Main clause + subordinate – any noun + would not + have + participle II

Jasper explained why <u>they would not have won</u> the competition.

would not = wouldn't

Jasper explained why they <u>wouldn't have won</u> the competition.
Джаспер объяснил, почему они не выиграли бы соревнование.

Dan said that he would never have pulled Sue's plaits,
if she hadn't pushed him.
Дэн сказал, что никогда не стал бы тянуть Сью за
косички, если бы она не толкнула его.

Questions: A) Put the question to the main clause
   B) Add the subordinate clause.

   Ivan knew Ken would have come.
   Did Ivan know that Ken would have come?

> 1. Did + noun + verb + (that) subordinate clause
> 2. Question word + did + noun + verb + (that)

| subordinate clause |
| --- |

<u>The children assured they would have made their gift for Ann by her birthday.</u>
Дети заверили, что сделают подарок для Энн к ее дню рождения.

Did the children assure that they would have made their gift for Ann by her birthday? – Yes, they did.
What did the children assure of? – That they would have made their gift for Ann by her birthday.
Who assured they would have made their gift for Ann by her birthday? – The children did.

<u>Jack insisted he would have accompanied Jill after the party.</u>
Джек настаивал, чтобы он проводил Джилл после вечеринки.

Did Jack insist that he would have accompanied Jill after the party? – Yes, he did.
What did Jack insist on? – That he would have accompanied Jill after the party.
Who insisted he would have accompanied Jill after the party? – Jack did.

The other day the engineer was sure that the construction would have been completed by the end of the month.

Was the engineer sure that the construction would have been completed by the end of the month? – Yes, he was.
Was the engineer sure that the construction would have been completed by the next day? – No, he wasn't.
Who was sure that the construction would have been completed by the end of the month? – The engineer was.
What was the engineer sure of? – That the construction would have been completed by the end of the month.

# Future Perfect Continuous in the Past

Let's remember the continuous tense: the action takes place at a certain time.

Present continuous: We <u>are watching</u> TV at night.
Мы смотрим телевизор ночью.

| be + verb + "ing" ending |
| --- |

Future continuous: Terry <u>will be watching</u> TV at night.
Терри будет смотреть телевизор ночью.

| will be + verb + ing |
| --- |

Perfect continuous:  Terry <u>have been watching</u> TV for 2 hours. Терри уже 2 часа смотрит телевизор.

| have been + verb-ing |
| --- |

Future perfect continuous: Terry <u>will have been watching</u> TV for 2 hours by the time I come.
К тому времени, как я приду, Терри будет смотреть телевизор уже 2 часа.

| will have been + verb-ing |
| --- |

Future perfect continuous in the past: Terry said that by my arrival he would have been watching the telly for 2 hours. Terry сказал, что до моего прихода он смотрел телик в течение 2 часов.

| would have been + verb-ing |
| --- |

We use "the future perfect continuous in the past" to describe the action, which:
1. started in the past
2. would continue for a certain period of time
3. would be finished before another action in the future

We usually use "the future perfect continuous in the past" for a sequence of tenses 1. In complex sentences
2. In reported speech.

Complex sentence = main clause + subordinate clause

The children assured they would have been making their gift for Ann by her birthday. - Дети заверили, что будут делать и сделают подарок Энн к ее дню рождения.

The main clause – noun/pronoun + verb in the past tense
The children assured

The subordinate clause – noun/pronoun + would + have been + participle I (by)

they would have been making their gift for Ann by her birthday.

Jack has insisted he would have been accompanying Jill after the party right to her door. Джек настоял, что после вечеринки он проводит Джилл прямо до ее двери.

Negative form: would not = wouldn't

subordinate clause – noun/pronoun + would not + have been + participle I

I was sure Tony would not have been training before the competition. Я был уверен, что Тони не тренировался до соревнований.
I was sure Tony wouldn't have been training before the competition.

Questions
We ask the question to the main clause, adding the subordinate one as it is.

1. Did + noun + verb + (that) subordinate clause
2. Question word + did + noun + verb + (that) subordinate clause

Nick said to me that they would have been playing for 15 minutes before the first goal.
Ник сказал мне, что они уже отыграли 15 минут до первого гола.

Did Nick say they would have been playing for 15 minutes before the first goal? – Yes, he did.
Who said that they would have been playing for 15 minutes before the first goal? – Nick did.
Whom did Nick say they would have been playing for 15 minutes before the first goal? – He said it to me.
Whom did Nick say it to? – To me.

Yesterday Maurine told me that they would have been living in Hastings for 20 years by the end of March.
Морин сказала мне, что к концу марта они прожили бы в Хейстингсе 20 лет.

Who told you that they would have been living in Hastings for 20 years by the end of March? – Maurine did.
Did Maurine tell you they would have been living in Hastings for 20 years by the end of March? – Yes, she did.
When did Maurine tell you that they would have been living in Hastings for 20 years by the end of March? – She told me yesterday.
Whom did she tell that they would have been living in Hastings for 20 years by the end of March? – To me.
Who did she tell it to? – She told it to me.
Did Maurine or her husband tell you that they would have been living in Hastings for 20 years by the end of March? – Maurine did.

# Sentences

Sentence – предложение, изречение, сентенция

## Functions in the sentence

Subject – подлежащее, Predicate – сказуемое
Object – дополнение, Attribute – определение
Adverbial – обстоятельство, Adverb – наречие

## Simple sentence

A simple sentence is a clause, which consists of one subject and one predicate. It is one independent clause.
We put a dot at the end of the sentence.

I am teaching you. I teach you English.
I have been teaching English for many years.
I have taught you nearly everything I knew.

## Compound sentence

Clause – предложение
Comma – запятая (,)
Colon – двоеточие (:)
Semicolon – точка с запятой (;)
Dot = full stop – точка

The compound sentence consists of two or more clauses, relative to each other. The clauses are usually joined by conjunctions or by comma, colon or semicolon.

| Compound sentence = clause + conjunction + clause |
| --- |

I invited Jane and she is coming at 10 o'clock.
(2 subjects and 2 predicates)

We shall go out whenever Tom is ready.
I am speaking to you and you are listening to me.
I am speaking to you but you are not listening to me.

# Complex sentence

Main clause = Principal clause – главное предложение
Subordinate clause – придаточное предложение

The complex sentence consists of the principal (main) clause and one or more subordinate clauses. The subordinate clauses are joined to the principal clause by conjunctions.

| Complex sentence = main clause + subordinate clause |
| --- |

This is the woman, <u>whom</u> I love.
The woman, <u>who</u> is standing by the piano, is the one <u>that</u> I love.

The principal clause is independent and can function on its own; "This is the woman," – is a principal clause; it's an independent sentence: This is the woman. "whom I love." – is a subordinate, dependent clause with no sense, characterizing the woman.

Subordinate clauses are dependent and cannot function on their own; they explain the gist of the main clause or add more information. Each subordinate clause must have a subject and a predicate.

There are several types of subordinate clauses.

Principal (main) clause
/ \
subordinate clauses
/ \
adjective, noun, adverbial, pronoun, condition, time

That's the book I want to read. – Adjective clause
Toby said that he was very tired. – Noun clause
He ran away <u>when he saw the policeman</u>. – Time clause
We can go there <u>if you wish to</u>. – Condition clause
As soon as Jasper heard me, he rushed into my open hands. – Adverbial clause
Please, return the book, <u>which I gave you a month ago</u>. – Relative pronoun clause

# Adjective Clause

An adjective clause describes a noun in the main clause. Adjective clauses function as adjectives:

The car, <u>which was red,</u> belonged to the Blakes.

There are two main kinds of an adjective clause:

      1. Non-defining clauses, which give extra information about the noun. They are not essential (не существенны):

The desk in the corner, <u>which is covered in books,</u> is mine.
", which is covered in books, - this information isn't very important;
"The desk in the corner is mine". – There is sense here; we can understand which table we refer to. - Defining clause

      2. Defining clauses give essential information about the noun:

The parcel, that I've just received, is on your desk.
", that I've just received," – this information is important.

      The conjunctions of adjective clauses:

We use "which, that, when, where, whose" to subordinate an adjective clause.

We use "who, whom, that", if the adjective clause describes a person.

## Relative Pronoun Clause

We use a relative pronoun to introduce an adjective clause:

The main relative pronouns: who, whom, which, that

"who" – for humans in subject position.

Elizabeth, who is sitting opposite you, is my girlfriend.

"whom" – for humans in object position.

The girl, whom you see opposite you, is Elizabeth, my girlfriend.

"which" – for things and animals in subject or object position.

We've bought a flat, which needs redecoration.
We have a dog, which greets my friends with a handshake".

"that" – for humans, animals and things, in subject or object position.

We are redecorating the flat that we have recently bought.
This is the man that has stolen my purse.

### Noun Clause

A noun clause is a subordinate clause, which acts as a noun.

Noun clauses usually start with conjunctions "how, that, what, whatever, when, where, whether, which, whichever, who, whoever, whom, whomever, why".

Noun clauses can function as subjects, objects or appositives (rename the noun next to it).

I remembered that Tom, what a thorough boy he was even when a child, had asked me to phone you. – subject

Clare was shocked with what she had seen. – object
My fluffy kitten, naughty creature, likes sleeping on my bed. – appositive

My sister, a student of the university, is a real beauty. – appositive

## Adverbial Clause

The adverbial clause functions as an adverb in a sentence.

As other clauses, it has a subject and a predicate.

Adverbial clauses add the information about the action in the sentence: when, where, why, how, under what condition it takes place.

Adverbial subordinate clauses can begin with the following conjunctions: after, although, because, if.

I asked you to talk to her, because I trusted you.
We shall be late, unless we take a taxi.
Although Ann was a teacher by profession, she was working as a secretary.
I will start only after all the managers are present.
We must make a reservation for accommodation before we leave.
I am deeply in love with her since the very first meeting.

## "When" Clause

"When" clause is the clause of time - for sure, which means we are sure that the action will take place, but we are not certain about the time.

I will let you know when I am coming.

"when I am coming" = I am definitely coming, but I am not sure when.

Are you coming or not? – I'll call you when I know the exact time.

We shall have tea when you come back.

When you receive the message, read it attentively.

# Conditional Clause

**"If"** clause is the clause of condition.

If I come to you, = it is possible, but I am not sure.
Will you come or not? – <u>If I decide to come</u>, I'll call you.

"If" can be at the beginning or in the middle of a sentence.

If we go by bus, it will be cheaper. =
It will be cheaper if we go by bus.

If you don't hurry, we shall miss the train. =
We shall miss the train if you don't hurry.

After "if" we use the verb in present (no "will").
If you see (not if you will see)

<u>If</u> I get home this evening, it'll be very late.
<u>If</u> I am late this evening, don't wait for me.

We are going to sunbathe <u>if</u> the weather is sunny.
We won't go if it is promised to be rainy.

If you are hungry, have something to eat.
If the phone rings, will you please answer it?

Do you mind, if I use your phone?
If I don't feel well tomorrow, I will stay at home.

Are you going to the concert? – Yes, if I can get a ticket.
I am going to the concert if I can get a ticket.

Will you go to the party, if they invite you? – If they invite me,
I will certainly go there.

## "If / when" + verb in present indefinite

If we decide to go to the forest, I shall tell you.
When we decide to go to the forest, I shall tell you.

But: Tell me if you will watch the film. Tell me when you will watch the film. - These are not complex sentences with "if/when" clauses.

The subordinate clause contains both: a subject and a predicate.

*Compare and analyse*:

A) 1. When do you come home from work?
   2. Tell me when you will come home.
   3. When you come home, you will see a surprise. – complex sentence

B) 1. I want to know when you will ring me up.
   2. When you receive this letter, I shall be far away. – complex sentence
   3. When do you have your appointment?

C) 1. I want you to tell me if you have enough money.
Я хочу, чтобы ты сказал мне, достаточно ли у тебя денег.

   2. I shall do that if I have time. – complex sentence
Я сделаю это, если у меня будет время.

   3. My mum asks me if I shall go with you to the forest.
Моя мама спрашивает, пойду ли я с тобой в лес.

Read the examples of "if / when" clauses:

We shall go shopping when the fridge is empty.
I will explain it again if you do not understand.
If the task is difficult, I will ask you how to do it.
When the dinner is ready, the nanny will give us a shout.
When I know English well, I will read books in English.
If I have time, I'll come to see you on Sunday.
If I finish my work soon, we shall go for a walk.

Questions:

Who goes shopping when your mother is ill?
What will your friends do when they have their holidays?
Where will you spend next Sunday, if the weather is rainy?
What book will you take at the library, when you go there next time?

### If I had
Если бы у меня было

Dan likes fast cars but he doesn't have one.
He doesn't have enough money.
If he had the money, he would buy a fast car.
Если бы у него были деньги, он бы купил скоростной
автомобиль.

Usually "had" is the past tense,
but in the above sentence "had" is not the past tense.

If he had the money = если бы у него были деньги
if he had the money now (but he doesn't have money)
если бы у него были деньги сейчас (но у него нет денег)

You can say: If he had the money, he would buy a car. =
He would buy a car if he had the money.

> If he had +  he would + buy
> If subject had + subject would + verb

I don't know the answer. If I knew the answer, I would tell you.
It's raining, so we are not going out. We would get wet if we went out.
I am sorry, I can't help you. I'd help you if I could.
If we had a car, we could travel more.
If I had time, I would go with you today.

# If / were

If I were … Если бы я был    /    If he, she, you, they were …

"were" – in the conditional clause is not the past tense of the verb "to be". It is a subjunctive (сослагательное наклонение) –

If I were …, I would …

If I were you … На твоем месте

"If I were you"- we use it to give advice; what you would do under the same circumstances.

If  I were + noun/pronoun + I would + verb + …

Tom: I failed the exam.
Lizzy: If I were you, I would learn grammar more seriously.

Kerry: My purse has been stolen.
Glen: If I were you, I would keep the purse in the inner pocket.

My girl-friend left me. What would you do, if you were me?
If I were you, I would consider whether I really need her.

"If I were a king," - Если бы я был королем, but I am not a king.
"If I were president", - Если бы я был президентом,

*Pay attention to the tenses in the "if" clauses and compare them with the tenses in the "I would" clauses.*

If I were president I would cut the cost of education.
Если бы я был президентом, я бы сократил расходы на образование.

If I had been president, I would have cut the cost of education.
If I were elected president next year, I would cut the cost of education.
Если бы меня избрали президентом в следующем году, я бы сократил расходы на образование.

If he asks me, I will help him. – open conditional

If he asked me, I would help him. – subjunctive conditional past

If he had asked me, I would have helped him. – subjunctive conditional perfect

Negative sentences: would not

| If I were + noun/pronoun + I would not + verb + … |
| --- |

If I were president, I would not raise taxes.
If I had been president, I would not have raised taxes.
If I were elected president, I wouldn't sign the tax increase next week.

It's warm; if I were you, I wouldn't put the coat on.
It's not a very nice place. I wouldn't go there if I were you.
It wouldn't be nice if the weather were (was) worsening.
If there was a good film on TV, we wouldn't go out.

Questions

| 1. "If were" clause + (what) would + noun/pronoun + verb + |
| --- |
| 2. Would + noun/pronoun + verb +"if were" clause |
| 3. What would + noun/pronoun + verb +"if were" clause |

If you were jobless, what would you do?
If there wasn't so much traffic, could we drive faster?
Would we travel very much, if I hadn't got a car?
Would Sue enjoy her work, if she didn't like it?
Could we better go out, if you stop watching telly?
Would you rather play chess, if you want to quicken your brains?
Wouldn't be the world a better place, if there were no wars on the Earth?

# Indirect speech

## Indirect commands and requests

The indirect speech is the speech, which tells what someone said.

Transforming direct speech into reported one, you can use the words: said, told, informed, admitted, claimed, confirmed, replied, explained, asked, wondered, worried, wanted to know, was / were eager to know

Father – to his son: Pass me the sugar, please
Father asks his son to pass him the sugar.

Steve – to his brother: I shall go to the library.
Steve informs his brother that he will go to the library.

Kerry: "Ken, close the door please" –
Kerry wanted Ken to close the door.

Toby: "Stand still, boys" – Toby ordered the boys to stand still.

He ordered us to close the door.
She told us not to waste the time.
He advised us not to drive that way.

## Present tense

Andy: "I don't want to go there" – Direct speech of Andy.

Andy says he does not want to go there. – Indirect (reported) speech.

*Read and compare the direct and reported speech.*
*Pay attention to the changes in the reported speech.*

Jimmy: "It's so cold in the room." –
He says that it's very cold in the room.

1. The name "Jimmy" is changed for the pronoun "He".
2. We changed the exclamation "so" into the adverb "very"
3. "He says" – present tense; that's why the transformed direct speech is remaining in the same tense.

Clare: "I am very tired today"– She says she's very tired.

4. You can use the conjunction **"that"** or can miss it.

Mr. Blake says they usually go on holiday in the summer.
What does Mr. Blake say? You can answer:

a) Mr. Blake says they usually go on holiday in the summer.
b) Mr. Blake says that they usually go on holiday in the summer.

> Sam: "Our plane will take off on time" –
> Sam says (that) their plane will take off on time.
>
> Betty: "I flew to Madrid by KLM last month. –
> Betty says she flew to Madrid by KLM last month.

5. While transforming the direct questions into reported, we change the question form into a positive statement.

Billy: "What discount can you give me, Luis?" (can you?)
Billy asks what discount Luis can give him. (Luis can)

The manager: "Why did you send the parcel so late? –
The manager asks why we sent the parcel so late.

John: "When will Luis come to London?" –
John would like to know when Luis comes to London.

"How long have you known Billy?" –
I wonder how long you have known Billy.

> Examples of reported speech:

She wants to know where you spent your holidays.
He says that he is reading a book.

She confirms that they have just come.
He is eager to know who has come.
The policeman notifies the girl not to cross the street there.


## Past tense

*Read and pay attention to the sequence of tenses in the past.*

Christine – to her sister: Please <u>do not leave</u> the door open.
Christine <u>asked</u> her sister <u>not to leave</u> the door open.

Father – to his son: Pass me the sugar, please
Father asked his son to pass him the sugar.

Steve – to his brother: I <u>shall</u> go to the library.
Steve informed his brother that he <u>should</u> go to the library.

1. We can consider the reported speech as a complex sentence.

Ann – to her friend: <u>Do you like</u> my new dress?
<u>Ann asked</u> her friend <u>whether she liked</u> her new dress.

"Ann asked her friend" – past tense.
The direct question "Do you like my new dress?" (present tense)
is transformed into reported speech in the past tense.

Nancy – to her partner: Where are you going on holiday?
Nancy wanted to know where her partner was going on holiday.
Nancy was curious to know where her partner was going on holiday.
Nancy was eager to know where her partner was going on holiday.

Helen - to her mum:  I have lost my umbrella.
Helen told her mum that she had lost her umbrella.
(Present perfect tense is changed into past perfect)

Teacher – to pupils: Who is absent?
The teacher asked the pupils who was absent.
The teacher wanted to know who of the pupils was absent.

Trevor: I am tired.
a) What did Trevor say to you? – He said he was tired.
b) What did he tell you? – He told me that he was tired.

You can say: He said that he was tired. *or*
He said he was tired.

Ann told me that she didn't like her job. *or*
Ann told me she didn't like her job.

*Study how to transform the direct speech into the reported one in the past tense.*

| | |
|---|---|
| This → That | These → Those |
| Here → There | Now → Then |
| Today → That day | This week → That week |
| Tomorrow → The next day | Yesterday → The previous day |

*Study how the verbs are changed in the reported speech in the past tense.*

| | |
|---|---|
| am / is → was | are → were |
| have / has → had | can → could |
| will → would | do / does → did |
| look → looked | feel → felt |

*Read what friends told about themselves when they met at the party: mind how the sentences and tenses are changed.*

Sarah: We're going to buy a house.
Sarah said they were going to buy a house.

Diana: I am enjoying my new job.
Diana said that she was enjoying her new job.

My father isn't very well.
She said her father wasn't very well.

Peter: I have to go early. Peter said he had to go early.

Clark: My sister has gone to Canada.
He said his sister had gone to Canada.

Ann: I can't find a job.
Ann said that she couldn't find any job.

Steve: I'll phone you. Steve said he would phone me.

Angela: I don't like my job. My son doesn't like school.
Angela said that she didn't like her job and her son did
not like school.

Mike: You look tired. Mike said that I looked tired.
I replied: I feel fine. I replied that I felt fine.

# Idiomatic expressions

I'm pretty sure. = I am quite sure. Я совершенно уверен.
Take a bath = have a bath (a shower). Принимать ванну (душ).

On the trains, you can hear some announcements (объявления)
In the shops (other places) you can see the following notes.

Keep silence. Соблюдайте тишину.
Keep left. Держитесь левой стороны.
Keep right. Держитесь правой стороны.
Keep in mind – remember.

Mind the step. Обратите внимание (имейте в виду) - ступенька.
Mind the gap. Осторожно, щель, проём между вагоном и платформой.

Mind your head. Берегите голову. (садясь в такси)
Mind you. Имейте в виду. - Mind you, I'll check when you leave.

Do me a favour please. Сделай мне одолжение, пожалуйста.
Will (could) you do me a favour, please?
Не могли бы вы сделать мне одолжение, пожалуйста?

### "Bring" приносить
He was brought up (educated, trained) - Он был воспитан
What brings you here? = Why have you come here?
His work has brought him fame and riches.
Bring back = give back, return.
Bring back happy days – remind.
The jury brought in a verdict.
Присяжные вынесли вердикт.

### "Bare" = naked голый
Barefoot – shoeless – босоногий
Bareheaded – uncovered (no hat)

"used to …" – we use it for a repeated action in the past, which is finished now.
I used to go to the forest every day, but I don't go now.

He used to have dinner with friends, but he doesn't do it now.
Dave used to work at a factory. Now he works at a supermarket.

By the way – кстати, между прочим

As soon as I can – Как только смогу. – Thank you for your request. I will answer it as soon as I can.

Agree with somebody – I absolutely agree with you.
Agree to something – I agree to your terms.

Put off – postpone
Never put off till tomorrow what you can do today.

### Expressions for shopping
Use by ... Использовать в / до
Best before ... Употребить до
Sell by ... Годен до
The date of expiry ... Срок годности

### Standard structures: "I want you to …" я хочу чтобы ты
I want somebody to do something.

I want you to enter the university.
Sue wants me to clean the carpet.
I wanted Tom to meet me.
Do you want me to help you?
I don't want you to be present at the party.

### "It takes" - Занимает

It takes me some time. Это займет у меня некоторое время.
It takes me 30 minutes to get to work.
How long does it take you to get to work? – 30 minutes.
It takes mum two hours to clean the rooms.
It will take you only a minute to look through this phrase.
It has taken me 2 hours to fly to Heathrow.
How long has it taken you to fly to Heathrow? – 2 hours.

# Credits

Cover: Illustration 82951819 © creativecommonsstockphotos - Dreamstime.com. Big Ben clock tower and Parliament Building with London Eye against blue skies.

Printed in Great Britain
by Amazon